WHY BUY BITCOIN

INVESTING TODAY IN THE MONEY OF TOMORROW

ANDY EDSTROM

COUNTERCYCLE MEDIA

Countercycle Media
Los Angeles, California U.S.A.
www.countercyclemedia.com
www.andyedstrom.com

Library of Congress Control Number: 2019946247

Publisher's Cataloging-In-Publication Data
(Prepared by The Donohue Group, Inc.)

Names: Edstrom, Andy, author.
Title: Why buy bitcoin : investing today in the money of tomorrow / Andy
    Edstrom, CFA, CFP.
Description: First edition. | Los Angeles, California : Countercycle Media,
    2019. | Includes bibliographical references and index.
Identifiers: ISBN 9781733219600 | ISBN 9781733219617 (Kindle) | ISBN
    9781733219624 (ePub)
Subjects: LCSH: Bitcoin. | Money--History. | Investments.
Classification: LCC HG1710 .E37 2019 (print) | LCC HG1710 (ebook) |
    DDC 332.178--dc23

Edited by Beth Rashbaum
Cover design by Lance Buckley
Author photo by Kenchy Ragsdale
Formatting by Brenda Van Niekerk
Production by AuthorFriendly.com

Printed in the USA
First Edition, August 2019

To Joanna

Beautiful, loving, brilliant, supportive, tireless

Contents

Table of Figures

Preface

Why You Should Care

Magical Internet Money Fails to Go Away

Most people who encounter Bitcoin initially dismiss it out of hand. "Magical Internet Money" sounds like a wacky idea. I remember my own first exposure to Bitcoin clearly. I was on vacation with my wife and my nine-month-old son. Driving from Vienna to Budapest, I was listening to a podcast of my favorite periodical, *The Economist*.[1] It was April 2013, and in its four years of existence Bitcoin had already experienced its first price bubble and crash. At the time Bitcoin was the first and only cryptocurrency with any significant market traction. Internet-native money struck me as a bizarre concept, and I paid it no heed. Bitcoin's price at the time was around $180. As of this writing, it is around $8,500, representing a gain of roughly 4,600%. Oops.

The second time I remember encountering Bitcoin and cryptocurrencies was reading an article in *The Wall Street Journal* in July 2016[2] that discussed the "hard fork" that split another cryptocurrency, Ethereum, in two. A similar fate would also befall Bitcoin two years later. Ethereum was a putative competitor to Bitcoin that seemed even wackier than Bitcoin itself. It wasn't obvious to me why geeks were experimenting with this stuff, so again I ignored it. At the time Ethereum's price was around $12. As of this writing it's around $255, representing a gain of roughly 2,000%. Oops again.

The third time I encountered Bitcoin and cryptocurrencies was in early 2017 when a friend who had started an artificial intelligence-based company forwarded me some materials from a friend of his who was raising money to start a crypto-focused hedge fund. That got my attention. I had spent most of my career as an investor, and launching a fund is something every professional investor dreams of. Launching a fund is a ticket to the big leagues of professional investing. Launching a fund to invest in assets that were trying to be money (cryptocurrencies) was an interesting idea.

By that time the total cryptocurrency market capitalization had reached tens of billions of dollars and was still rising rapidly. Bitcoin's share of the total market capitalization, which had been around 80% for several years, was falling as other cryptocurrencies were bid up at an even faster rate than Bitcoin was. Something interesting was going on here. It was either a very interesting investment opportunity, a bubble, or a scam. It ended up being a combination of all three.

Monetary Technological Disruption

As an investor, I have always been fascinated by the prospect of either finding an asset worth $1 today that I could buy for 50 cents ("value" investing) or an asset worth $1 today that had a reasonable shot of being worth $10 years in the future ("growth" investing). Most of my professional experience involved investing in assets that generated cash flows and had what Benjamin Graham and David Dodd, the fathers of value investing, called "intrinsic value."[3] And I have done well at this kind of value investing. But despite my success, I had a lot to learn.

A college degree in Economics, two professional financial certifications (CFA and CFP), and a decade and a half of professional investment, asset allocation, and financial advisory experience provided me with a rich set of tools and experiences with which to understand the financial world. Yet it left me without the most fundamental understanding of money. I need to underscore this. *I managed to spend tens of thousands of hours of my life working directly with money without gaining an understanding of its core underlying fundamentals.* If the core fundamentals of money eluded a financial professional like me for so long, I can have some confidence that they have likewise eluded others, probably including you.

Like a financial professional today who doesn't really understand money, I suppose that a horse breeder in the nineteenth century didn't understand the underlying physical mechanics and engineering that made horses an effective source of locomotive power to passenger- and package-carrying buggies. Such a lack of understanding would not have prevented the horse breeder from making a respectable living—until the arrival of the automobile revolution, which decimated the demand for horses and therefore his livelihood.[4] History is full of examples of new technologies disrupting existing industries and creating new winners at the expense of the losers. It is also full of examples of those who don't understand the vast potential of these new technologies.

In 1998, almost a century after the automobile came into use, economist Paul Krugman wrote in the popular Internet bubble-era magazine *The Red Herring* that "by 2005 or so it will become clear that the Internet's impact on the economy has been no greater than the fax machine's."[5] A decade later Krugman won the Nobel Prize in economics. But another decade after that, his Internet prognostication now ranks as one of the most ridiculous predictions in modern economic history. Like other skeptics of the era, Krugman evidently didn't anticipate companies like Alibaba, Amazon, Apple, Facebook, Google, Netflix, Tencent, and others. These Internet-native companies have had a gargantuan effect on the global economy and created trillions of dollars of stock market capitalization, while dramatically impacting civil society. And they have had a huge effect on the magazine and newspaper industry, which Krugman, who writes a regular newspaper column, would undoubtedly be the first to admit. Like Krugman, many newspaper publishers didn't imagine how the Internet would divert readers' attention to other news platforms, take away their classified ads business, gut their newsrooms, and eviscerate their profits.

The example of what happened to the traditional press industry is particularly salient to Bitcoin because, like the websites and attention aggregators that crippled the newspapers, Bitcoin is native to the Internet. Internet-based disruptions tend to happen rapidly—much more rapidly than when the car disrupted the horse a century ago. Helping people avoid the surprising level of disruption that could be caused by the arrival of a new technology for money is one thing that motivated me to write this book.

Another motivation is the financial opportunity that investing in this new technology could bring. Avoiding being on the losing side of a new monetary technology is reason enough to attempt to understand the underlying fundamentals of money and the potential threat posed by a new and better form of money. But if avoiding the losing side is interesting, so is joining the winning side. At minimum, it may make sense for some people to "hedge their bets" by gaining a modest amount of *positive* exposure to this potential disruption. Beyond that, I believe that Bitcoin has the potential to undo some of the massively regressive effects of our current economic system and partially mitigate some of the wealth imbalances this system has created.

Getting the Basics

Learning the underlying fundamentals of money has taken me hundreds of hours of research and reflection. Understanding the "new technology" of Bitcoin and cryptocurrency has taken thousands of hours more. I still learn something new about it almost every day. I have attempted to help my colleagues, clients, and friends to understand the fundamentals of money and how Bitcoin is poised to shake the foundations of the existing monetary system. I suspect my efforts have mostly failed.

This book is an attempt to remedy that failure. I flirted with the idea of subtitling this book *Bitcoin for Boomers* because many of my clients and family members are baby boomers who have not had the experience of "growing up online" as the millennial generation has. But I decided against it because I didn't want to restrict this book to a single age cohort. I wanted to present to *anyone* willing to open her mind the clearest case I could for why Bitcoin has a reasonable chance of becoming both the best money the world has ever known and an opportunity for a profitable investment.

I don't expect to impart a deep *technical* understanding of Bitcoin to readers any more than I expect them to understand the TCP-IP protocols that govern how information transits the Internet today. But just as a basic understanding of cloud computing, network effects, and the economics of human attention (i.e., "monetizing eyeballs") provides an understanding of how the giant Internet companies work, so can a fundamental grasp of money lead to an understanding of Bitcoin's potential to compete with the money we use today. I hope this book is accessible enough to start you on your journey to understanding Bitcoin's potential, because if that potential is realized, Bitcoin could reorganize the world's financial system and accrue *trillions* of dollars of value, representing an increase of perhaps 50x its current price over the next decade.

The Framework

Although this book is ultimately about Bitcoin, it's also about money. This reflects my personal journey, which included (1) attempting to understand Bitcoin, (2) attempting to understand the wider world of cryptocurrencies, (3) pivoting to trying to understand money, and finally (4) understanding Bitcoin. This journey was long and arduous, and one key goal of this book is to put the reader on a more direct path. Therefore, this book will attempt to address (1) why money is important, (2) what money is (fundamentally), (3) the current state of the world of money and debt, (4) what Bitcoin offers as an investment, and (5) Bitcoin's risks.

Warning to Readers

Before we begin, I offer a few cautionary words. This examination of the monetary world seeks truth. I have written it from the point of view of an investor, and in the world of investing, when reality collides with courtesy, it is courtesy that gives way. Reading this book may cause you to question some fundamentally held but insufficiently examined assumptions about the world. I hope it improves your understanding, but please be aware that it may cause some psychological discomfort. To those unwilling to suffer some anxiety, return this book to Amazon! To the intrepid truth seekers, read onward!

Chapter 1

Why Is Money?

I recall that my parents started giving me an allowance around age seven. We had just moved down the street to a slightly larger house in order to accommodate my newborn baby brother. If having a little brother came with cash flow, that was okay with me! I remember a piggybank, and I remember the rule was that I had to save a certain percentage of my allowance in the piggybank. I also had to set aside a portion for charity. I learned that saved money held the possibility of future purchases. Thanks to my parents' piggybank policy, saving money was firmly embedded in my character by the time I reached high school.

When I took Economics 101 as a college freshman I loved it, but I was surprised at its cursory treatment of money. It noted that money was (1) a medium of exchange, (2) a store of value, and (3) a unit of account. But none of what I learned illuminated why money exists in the first place and what fundamentally gives it value. We will do better. Before we can understand why Bitcoin has the potential to become the world's best money, we must understand what makes something good money. This requires us to first briefly review why money exists at all.

The Problem of Transacting

Another thing my college economics textbook taught me was that money was the solution to the primitive practice of barter. In his classic *An Inquiry into the Nature and Causes of the Wealth of Nations*, Adam Smith describes a scenario in which a baker living prior to the invention of money wants a butcher's meat but has nothing that the butcher wants in exchange.[6] This situation lacks what has become known as the "double coincidence of wants" in which one party wants what the other party has and vice versa. Without such a double coincidence of wants, no commerce occurs, and economic growth is therefore stifled.

It's an appealing idea, and it sounds plausible. Yet, there's little or no evidence of the actual use of barter at scale in human history. David Graeber's opus *Debt: The First 5,000 Years* presents the evidence (or rather notes the lack of evidence) for barter in primitive societies.[7] More likely, such early economies didn't rely on barter at all, but rather relied on debt. It's easy to see why.

Suppose you are living in an early agricultural society. You will probably live out your entire life within a few miles of your birthplace. You are partly self-sufficient, but the advent of agriculture has created some food surplus and allowed modest capital accumulation, mostly in the form of physical structures, tools for agriculture and animal husbandry, garments, basic housewares, and weapons for defense of the community. Suppose you are planning a feast and you need a lamb to serve your family. Your neighbor has one he can spare, but the only surplus good you have is grain, and your neighbor doesn't need any grain at the moment. You face Adam Smith's double coincidence of wants problem.

"No problem," says your neighbor, "you can pay me back later." You and your neighbor have just created debt. This debt is a liability to you and an asset to your neighbor. Once you have a lamb or something of approximately equivalent or slightly greater value (the latter case implying a rate of return paid to the lender known as "interest"), you can settle the debt. The beauty of this system is that it is very low friction because you have a bond of trust with your neighbor. Since you live nearby and since people in such societies don't move frequently (or possibly ever), your neighbor knows you are unlikely to skip town and renege on the debt. Moreover, everyone knows everyone in the settlement, and if you default on your debt to your neighbor, your reputation will be stained. This will impair your ability to transact with others in the neighborhood in the future. The potential loss of your ability to transact with others in the future due to reputational damage is a significant potential cost to you.

Today these social costs of default are one of the key reasons that "microloans" in poor countries such as Bangladesh have very low default rates. Most of these loans get repaid despite the fact that the sums borrowed are often substantial to the borrowers (these loans aren't "micro" to them!), and despite the fact that this credit is sometimes used for risky business ventures that don't pay off and leave the borrower in a difficult financial position. In order to avoid the reputational risk of reneging on the debt, these borrowers move heaven and earth to find ways to repay their neighbors. For good or ill, social pressure from family and the community is very effective in deterring deadbeats![8]

Even in rich countries we still sometimes create and later settle small debts. Near my former office, I used to pick up a salad to eat at my desk when I didn't have time for a social or business lunch (a frequent occurrence). I always ordered the same salad from the café a block away, and when I went to pick it up, I always paid the proprietor, Lily, in cash. There was one form of payment that Lily didn't appreciate: credit cards. That's because she had to pay a percentage to the credit card processor, and she ran the risk of "chargebacks" due to fraudulent transactions (a topic we will return to later).

One day I showed up to pick up my salad, reached into my pocket, and realized I didn't have any cash on me. "Can I take the salad now and swing by later today with the payment?" I asked her. "Just pay me next time you come in for lunch," she offered. Given my long history of commerce with her, Lily knew there was a very high probability she'd get paid. Moreover, given the frequency of my lunch runs, she knew she wouldn't have to wait very long.

A decade before I went into debt for Lily's salad, I took a train from Albany, NY, to Grand Central Station in New York City one Saturday morning. I was a senior in college, the dot-com bubble had recently popped, and I was on my way to graduating into the worst job market in recent history. I was trying to convince Wall Street firms to hire me, even as those firms were laying off large numbers of their existing employees. Somehow I had landed an interview with a reputable Wall Street firm (yes, a few were still considered reputable at that time!), and I had timed my trip to New York so that I would have the weekend before my interview to spend with my girlfriend, who was there visiting her best friend. However, I was unable to reach her by phone when I arrived. Since I didn't know anyone else in the entire city and was intimidated by the idea of wandering around by myself, I hopped in a taxi after arriving at Grand Central Station and headed to a movie theater to kill some time.

As soon as the cab drove away, I realized I didn't have my wallet. I must have absent-mindedly left it on the seat after paying the driver. I had never been in a city so large and so imposing, and I was feeling overwhelmed. It also probably didn't help that my relationship with my girlfriend had been rocky lately. (A few months later we broke up.) I was stressed out and distracted, and it had cost me my wallet. And in a city of millions of people where I knew nobody, I wasn't going to find a Lily to feed me lunch on credit. This time I needed *money*.

Money Facilitates Societal Scaling

A few thousand years ago, even the biggest settlements were tiny compared to modern New York. But in agriculture-based hamlets and towns, the economics of specialization gradually changed the neighborly debt-based economy. Surplus generated by agriculture allowed greater portions of the population to specialize. The agricultural base could support blacksmiths, tanners, and jewelers, in addition to farmers and herders. Specialization brought dramatic increases in productivity via at least two factors.

First, productivity *per worker* increased with training and experience. The combined output of an experienced blacksmith, an experienced tanner, and an experienced farmer exceeded that of three people who each spent a third of their time smithing, tanning, and farming. This is because attaining expertise in a single trade resulted in higher productivity *per hour worked*. Second, specialization allowed some measure of matching talent with occupation. Perhaps the person with a better singing voice became an entertainer, while the one with a stronger back plowed the fields. When they were combined, specialization and talent sorting resulted in dramatic gains in productivity.

But such gains came with a greater reliance on commerce. The blacksmith was no longer self-sufficient and therefore had to trade with the tanner and the farmer.

When there were only a few professions, incurring debts with one's neighbors was efficient. But once multiple occupations differentiated and populations grew, transacting among neighbors and families became impractical.

Human relationships are famously limited to the "Dunbar Number."[9] Most people can't maintain personal relationships with more than about 150 people. So living in a town of 1,000 people with dozens of professions inevitably results in having to transact with some strangers. Living in a town of 10,000 people exacerbates the problem. Long before New York–sized cities emerged, people had to find a better way to conduct commercial transactions. Moreover, some goods weren't produced locally and had to be traded over distance between settlements. This resulted in more unknown faces. At scale, occupational specialization brings greater surplus and wealth to society. But it no longer works to incur and settle debts with all your trading partners. Many will be strangers, and you won't be able to trust each other.

Money solves the problem of transacting at greater levels of productivity and economic activity. It solves the problem of social scaling[10] and allows ever-greater levels of specialization, surplus generation, and wealth creation. In short, money is a key enabler of the enrichment and advancement of society. *It is therefore foundational to modern human civilization.* This is why it is so shocking that few people understand what money is.

I ended up getting the job at that reputable Wall Street firm. This was before the Global Financial Crisis of 2008–2009 when all of those firms (even the ones considered reputable by many, including the one I worked at) conspired to simultaneously enrich their senior employees while torpedoing the world economy. I was fortunate to leave Wall Street before the crisis hit and take a job at a firm specializing in investing in distressed companies on the other side of the country. The crisis blessed me with lots of interesting work in this area. And although we broke up for a time, I was also blessed by my girlfriend's decision to get back together, marry me, and bring me a beautiful family. But through it all, I ironically managed to spend almost 15 years working full-time (and more like double-time!) in the financial industry without gaining a deep understanding of one of its key pillars: money.

Chapter 2

What is Money?

While in college I saw a movie that became a cult classic—*Swingers*. One of the movie's most famous lines is spoken by a character giving a pep talk to his buddy, who is trying to work up his nerve to approach a girl at the bar. He tells him, "You're so 'money' and you don't even know it!" Before long, "money" became one of my generation's synonyms for "cool." That meant anyone and anything could be called "money." It took me almost two decades to understand that "everything being money" was actually true. This chapter will explain why money can thus be both a noun and an adjective.

Ludwig Von Mises is considered one of the most important economists in the Austrian school of economics. In his magnum opus, *Human Action*,[11] he distinguishes among three categories of goods that we might term: (1) consumption goods, (2) capital goods, and (3) money. Consumption goods are what we consume in everyday life. They include things like food and clothing. Capital goods are productive assets used to produce consumption goods. Factories, tools, and machines are capital goods. Because they are productive, capital goods deliver a rate of return for holding them. Distinct from both consumption goods and capital goods is *money*, which is a good that is used to transact among other goods, including consumption goods and capital goods. Fundamentally, it is what Mises' predecessor, influencer, and father of the Austrian school of economics Carl Menger called *a medium of exchange*.[12]

This framework is useful, but there are no absolutes, and the lines can blur. A building can be deployed as a capital good if it is filled with factory equipment, or it can be "consumed" over time as shelter if it is used as a house. A car can be used as a capital good to transport commodities for a profit-making business, or it can be used to drive to the beach and consume the associated entertainment. So buildings and vehicles can be part capital good and part consumption good. A pack of cigarettes can be consumed for pleasure or it can be traded for some other type of good. Likewise a bar of soap. These items are part consumption good and part money. A share of Apple stock represents part ownership of a profitable business and as such it delivers an investment return over time. And Apple stock is so liquid that it can be used to pay for something (if transferred between brokerage accounts). So, it is part capital good and part money.

Notwithstanding the blurred lines among consumption goods, capital goods, and money, the primary difference between money and capital goods is that a capital good generates a positive expected rate of return over time. However, this potential return comes at the cost of (1) risk of possible loss of value, and (2) lower liquidity (ability to transact). Having spent my career investing in both illiquid and liquid assets (both of which would be considered capital goods), I can tell you that liquidity is better than illiquidity. If I manage to accumulate wealth in excess of my daily needs and I can allocate some of this wealth to investments that I expect to generate a rate of return over time, then my wealth can "work" for me. But the future is uncertain, and some of my individual investments may turn bad. Or I might come across unanticipated investment opportunities at a later date that are more attractive than the ones in which I've already tied up my precious capital. Therefore, I prefer investments that are liquid, or easily *salable,* all else being equal.[13]

But all else isn't equal. Liquidity comes at a price. We see this in the price of liquid assets as compared to illiquid ones. Liquid assets trade at higher valuations (multiples of earnings and cash flow, etc.). For example, I may be able to buy a collection of apartment buildings at a multiple of 16x its annual cash flow. But such a transaction may take months to close (since these buildings aren't very liquid). If the same portfolio of apartment buildings is held by a REIT (real estate investment trust) that is publicly traded five days a week on the New York Stock Exchange, it may trade at a value of 20x its annual cash flow. This difference in valuation between 16x and 20x implies that the "monetary premium" embedded in the REIT is 4x cash flow (20x - 16x = 4x). This math implies that the REIT is effectively 80% "apartments" (capital goods) and 20% "money."

This same concept applies to consumption goods. Most consumption goods are liquid in the sense that they are easy to buy. However, most are harder to resell. This can be because a potential buyer suspects the reseller of trying to cheat him by trying to pass off a counterfeit or damaged good as an original. Or it may be for other reasons. Think about a ticket to a rock concert that you buy a month in advance. The concert is a consumption good. Suppose it's a big-name band and you are willing to pay $300 for it. Now suppose that a week before the concert, an emergency arises, and you can't make it to the show. $300 is a lot of money, and you can't afford to take the loss. Fortunately, you can put it up for sale on StubHub.com or sell it to a friend. Although the ticket is a "perishable" good, which will be worthless after the concert date, the fact that you can sell it and recover some value before then means this ticket has some monetary value.

Now consider a ticket for the same concert in a scenario in which the band doesn't want scalpers buying batches of tickets in advance. So the tickets are sold based on your individual identity and cannot be resold to another party at a later date. (This is how airline tickets generally work.) If you were willing to pay $300 for the concert ticket in the prior scenario in which you could resell it in an emergency, how much are you willing to pay for the ticket that you *can't* resell? Not $300, because if the emergency occurs, you won't be able to resell it and it will be worthless. Fortunately, you figure that the odds of the emergency occurring are pretty low, so you conclude that you're willing to pay $250 for the ticket. If this ticket that cannot be resold is worth $250 to you, and the ticket that *can* be resold is worth $300, then the value of the ticket that can be resold is effectively $250 "concert" and $50 "money."

Think about what you use as money today. It's probably a piece of paper that your government has told you is money. Ask yourself what you would use if it weren't available. If you live in a rich country like the United States, this may be a novel question. Consider yourself lucky! If you need some inspiration, ask your friend from Venezuela, Argentina, Zimbabwe, Cyprus, Russia, or Turkey. Or ask someone who's served time in prison. These folks can tell you that in a pinch, cigarettes or soap will do the trick. In parts of Africa cell phone minutes are commonly used as money. In these various cases, the consumption good that has a practical use can also be used as a medium of exchange. Cigarettes, soap, and cell phone minutes therefore have a monetary premium embedded in their overall value that is larger than what is found in most other consumption goods. This means that they are "more money" than most things.

This duality between the monetary (liquidity) value and the investment (capital) value, or between the monetary (liquidity) value and the consumption value, explains why money is an adjective as much as it is a noun. Just about everything is "a little bit money," and some things are more money than others. In practice, a bicycle is not very money, though it is a little bit money because it could be used as a medium of exchange if absolutely necessary. A share of Apple stock is more money than a house since the Apple stock is much more liquid. A dollar bill is more money than either. The share of the total value of a good that can be attributed to its monetary premium (its moneyness) ranges from 0%–100%, and this breakdown will be different for each and every capital good and consumption good.

A Clearer Definition of Money – Medium of Exchange

While everything is at least a little bit money, certain things are a lot more money—so much so that they become mostly used as money and therefore become known as "money." In a world without the "double coincidence of wants" problem identified earlier, consumption goods and capital goods might be the only two categories of goods we would think about. But building a complex economy with high levels of specialization that result in high levels of surplus requires a medium of exchange. Money is the medium that is the most liquid and salable of all. The seller of a capital good or a consumption good will accept money because she knows she can easily exchange it for another capital good or consumption good that she desires. Money is therefore the solution to the double coincidence of wants problem discussed earlier.

Being the best medium of exchange implies that the percentage of the money's total value that is attributable to its liquidity or moneyness is very high.

The best money has nearly 100% monetary value and near zero value as either a consumption good or a capital good. *Said differently, the best money is something that is useless as anything other than money.* In my exploration of money, this conclusion was one of the biggest surprises to me and possibly one of its least-understood truths. Many people argue that good money has an "intrinsic" or other industrial value, when in fact the opposite is true.

In his excellent book, *The Bitcoin Standard*, Austrian school economist Saifedean Ammous divides the double coincidence of wants problem into three categories: (1) location, (2) scale, and (3) time.[14] If you want to exchange an oak tree in one location for an almond tree in another location, you may struggle since trees aren't easily transferrable. This is a lack of double coincidence of wants across *location*. If you instead want to buy a book, you will struggle to pay for it using a car, since you can't easily slice off one book's worth of car. This is a lack of double coincidence of wants across *scale*. You may want to sell your house at what you deem an advantageous price, in exchange for a lifetime's supply of food. But since food is perishable, you will need to collect the food in pieces over a very long period of time rather than upfront. This is a lack of double coincidence of wants across *time*.

The definition of money as a medium of exchange that exhibits salability across distance, scale, and time comports with what I learned from my Econ 101 textbook, which defined money as (1) a medium of exchange, (2) a store of value, and (3) a unit of account. To say it's a "store of value" (pillar #2 of the Econ 101 textbook definition) is to recognize its property of being *salable across time*. Someone who holds money as a "store of value" wants to store that value so that she can transact with it later, thus solving the coincidence of wants problem across time. To describe money as a "unit of account" (pillar #3 of the Econ 101 Textbook Definition) is to acknowledge its use as the obvious common measure of value, something that will allow us to set an exchange for every kind of good, service, or transaction. Without money, all goods would have to be priced against each other in an unwieldy matrix of chickens per car, apples per house, and taxi rides per haircut. Instead, since money is half of every transaction, it's clearly simpler to use money as the measuring stick of value.

The insight that money's Econ 101 textbook definitions as (2) store of value, and (3) unit of account are just derivative of money's core use as (1) a medium of exchange, is important. But we need to go deeper, and we will do so in Chapter 4: What is Money *Really*? Before we do, we must set the stage against which we will pursue our deeper understanding of money. We need to frame the monetary world as it exists today. It may seem to be a stable, wealth-producing system. Certainly for the top 1% of earners and especially the top 0.1%, our current monetary system has proven to be successful (so far) beyond their wildest dreams. Yet it has profound flaws that contain the potential for disaster. For anyone who wants to know why Bitcoin is not just an attractive investment, but a tool with the potential to correct much of what is wrong with our global monetary system, the next three chapters are essential reading that will set the stage.

Chapter 3

Monetary Madness and Debt Debauchery

Modern Money versus Debt

In Chapter 1 we noted that the first medium of exchange was probably debt rather than money since it was easier for neighbors to simply "owe each other" for some time and "settle up later." We also observed that for specialization and the emergence of complex societies that generate large economic surplus and growing wealth, money was required. Of course, in our modern economy we have both debt and money. And we have a lot more debt than money.

In the modern world, debt is an agreement to pay money in the future in exchange for a good or service provided today. It allows a separation in *time* between Party A giving the good/service to Party B and Party B giving money to Party A. This is true for (1) a bar tab created in exchange for a beer, or (2) a company paying 30 days later for supplies delivered today, or (3) my IOU to Lily for the salad described in Chapter 1. All of these examples are debt created to facilitate the purchase of a consumption good, and in many cases such debts do not incur interest. In contrast, debts incurred to support purchases of capital goods almost always include a rate of return in the form of interest. In the case of a corporate loan or a real estate mortgage, debt can allow Party

A to access funds now in order to invest, earn a return on those funds, and pay back the original amount of money borrowed plus interest to Party B.

These different types of transactions are recombinations of a transaction involving consumption goods or capital goods in exchange for money, but with the added feature of a time delay. If payment of interest during the time interval is involved, then a rate of return is embedded, and the lender receives compensation for "time value." But the time delay (specifically the time elapsed between the first leg of the transaction and the later "settlement" of the transaction) also leads to risk of loss by the lender in the event that the party who is supposed to "settle up" in the future fails to do so.

Fractional Reserve Banking and Debt

Today most of the world's monetary system is based on "fiat currencies," such as the U.S. dollar. The label derives from the Latin word "fiat," which means "let it be done."[15] Fiat currencies are nominally bestowed with value by governments that effectively decree "let it be done," where "it" refers to a small piece of paper having an agreed-upon value in the economy. Although some scholars of money and currency differentiate between the terms "money" and "currency," I don't think this distinction is useful. I will therefore use these terms interchangeably in this book.

One of the key characteristics of this fiat currency system is that most of what we think of as "money" is actually being debt created by the banking system. When you deposit cash into your bank account, the bank takes the funds and lends most of them to a home buyer, a commercial real estate investor, or a business owner. The bank may have $100 million of deposits that it owes to its depositors like you. These depositors did, in fact, deposit $100 million of money, but the bank turns around and lends out $90 million and therefore only holds actual cash of $10 million to satisfy the $100 million of deposits. Then the borrowers who borrowed the $90 million from the bank take their borrowed money and deposit it in another bank. This bank holds $9 million as reserves and lends out the other $81 million to borrowers who, in turn, deposit it at other banks. The banks' process of taking demand deposits and lending the deposited money out to third parties has the effect of expanding what's known as the "money supply." Really this "money supply" is a combination of base money and the debt claims built on top of it. In the example above, $100 million of actual deposited cash is ultimately transformed into $1 billion of "money supply," which really comprises $100 million of base money and $900 million of *debt claims* on that deposited money. This 10x leverage (turning $1 into $10 of "money supply") is typical of the banking system in the United States and other developed countries. Moreover, because the central bank can print infinite amounts of money to guarantee the banks' deposits, the potential amount of money and associated debt is theoretically unlimited.

Unfortunately, this arrangement whereby the bank holds only a fraction of the deposits owed to its depositors in the form of cash reserves, is susceptible to a "bank run." In a system with 10x leverage, the bank can satisfy only the demands for 10% of depositors' cash. In his classic book *What has Government Done to Our Money?* Murray Rothbard notes that this arrangement is perhaps the only one in the world in which the seller of a service is allowed to promise to give the depositor her money "on demand" while knowing full well that the demand cannot actually be satisfied if more than a small fraction of depositors simultaneously make the demand.[16] In any other business, promising full availability of deposits on demand without actually holding a full inventory of such deposits would be considered fraud. Somehow the banking industry has managed to carve out for itself an exception to the usual rules of asset custody in which if you say you will hold an asset for someone, you actually have to hold it!

The banks can maintain this arrangement because they are backed by the central bank (the Federal Reserve in the United States), which has the ability to create "out of thin air" any amount of dollars required for banks to satisfy the demands of their depositors. This system contrasts starkly with a banking system based on gold or any other truly scarce base money that the central bank cannot print at will. In a gold-based system, any bank that issues deposits that exceed the reserves of gold in its vault risks a bank run, and the government won't be able to bail it out unless the government itself has gold reserves to fully back the gold-denominated deposits. This limits the amount of debt that can be created on top of the scarce base money.

The amount of *government* debt is similarly limited in a gold-based monetary system. That's because if the government has to repay its obligations in gold, it will have to accumulate enough reserves over time to satisfy its obligations. To understand the relationship between the type of base money (fiat dollars versus gold) and debt levels over time, take a look at total debt levels in the United States in the last century in Figure 1. The data have been illustrated ably by Ray Dalio, who runs Bridgewater Associates, the world's largest hedge fund.

The chart is specified in terms of Gross domestic product (GDP), which is the standard measure of total economic activity. The total debt in the economy as a percentage of gross domestic product (GDP) is measured on the right-side axis, and debt service is on the left-side axis. Debt service equals the sum of interest burden (percent of GDP that is paid in interest) and amortization (percent of GDP that is used to repay the outstanding debt principal balance).

A detailed world monetary history is beyond the scope of this book and has been ably covered by monetary historians. But here's a very short version of the last century. The numbered annotations in the chart correspond to the more detailed explanations in the following three paragraphs.

1. The first period of the last century saw a debt boom that helped fund the stock market mania of the 1920s. Overall debt levels rose in this period as investors and speculators "levered up" to maximize investment returns.

2. The stock market crash of 1929 and trade policy disasters such as the Smoot-Hawley tariffs of 1930 saw the economy collapse in 1930–1932, while debt levels remained elevated, resulting in rising debt/GDP.

3. FDR's election in late 1932 marked the turning point in debt/GDP levels, as New Deal policies ignited rapid economic growth while private sector debts continued to be written off. Debt/GDP decreased dramatically as debt (the numerator) fell and economic growth (the denominator) rose. Following the rise of fascism (itself caused partly by European and American economic policy errors in the 1920s and 1930s), the United States and countries of Western Europe found themselves embroiled in the largest war in history.

Figure 1: US Total Debt Burdens (% of GDP)

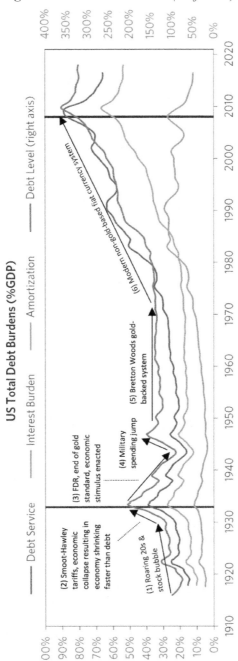

Data and Graph Source: A Template for Understanding Big Debt Crises, Ray Dalio, page 13; Text Source: Andy Edstrom

4. In 1943 U.S. military spending jumped and caused debt to rise more rapidly than overall economic growth, as citizens did their "patriotic duty" and bought government bonds while suffering rations on consumption goods.

5. By July 1944, as the tide of war turned against the Axis aggressors, treasury and monetary representatives of the United States and its European allies met in Bretton Woods, New Hampshire, to plan for a new world monetary standard that would foster peaceful economic development. Memorialized in the Bretton Woods Agreement, this arrangement essentially entailed the United States pegging the dollar to gold at a fixed rate, and the countries of Europe pegging their currencies to the dollar. This gold-based system lasted from 1945 to 1971. Given that it's much more difficult for overall debt levels to rise under such a gold-based monetary system, it's not surprising that this period saw relative stability in the United States' overall debt level and debt burden. You can see on the graph above that this was the most stable period for debt/GDP and debt service levels in the entire century. It was not to last.

6. When Richard Nixon announced the "temporary" (actually permanent) suspension of the Bretton Woods system on August 15, 1971, the United States embarked on the modern period of fiat currency in which the Federal Reserve was able to print unlimited amounts of new money. Almost immediately, the overall debt level began its multi-decade rise in which total debt/GDP exploded from roughly 145% to 350%! Note that these figures don't even include the largest debts owed by the U.S. government: unpaid Medicare and Social Security liabilities. The total present value of government debt including these obligations was estimated by economist Lawrence Kotlikoff to be $210 trillion back in 2014[17] and has been rising since then. That's roughly 1,000% of GDP in addition to the 350% for other debt in the economy. Debt levels in countries across the world have largely followed a similar path.

Although the chart clearly shows a peak in debt burdens in the 1930s and then a much higher more recent peak in 2008, there is a major difference between the resolution of the debt peak in the 1930s and the debt peak of 2008. In the 1930s, the debt burden in the U.S. fell significantly—due partly to mass defaults and partly to rapid economic growth from government stimulus. By contrast, the 2008 peak in debt has been only slightly reduced from about 350% of GDP in 2008 to 325% today. In the Global Financial Crisis of 2008–2009, debts were mostly preserved, though large portions were effectively transferred to the federal government's balance sheet as it printed money, funded huge budget deficits, and guaranteed the liabilities of banks, their counterparties (such as insurer AIG), and the giant publicly traded and supposedly (but not actually) "independent" mortgage guarantors, Fannie Mae and Freddie Mac.

So not only is the peak 350% of GDP debt level reached in 2008 much higher than the peak 200% of GDP reached in the 1930s, but, as the graph shows, the deleveraging that started a decade ago didn't get very far before slowing down and levelling out at a much higher percentage than in the prior cycle. Total debt falling from 350% of GDP to 325% hardly counts as a "deleveraging." The U.S. economy still has far more debt than at almost any time in the last century, and as of this writing the annual Federal budget deficit is set to hit $900 billion in 2019 and exceed $1 trillion annually in all years starting in 2022.[18] With total GDP of roughly $20 trillion, such deficits will increase the debt to GDP ratio at a rate of 5% annually, which will bring us back to record levels and beyond.

Note that these figures come from the federal government itself. So the picture may be much more dire than the one I've just painted. Asking the government to estimate its long-term budget is like asking my six-year-old how much candy he plans to eat this week. The response will always be skewed toward underestimation. Also, this ongoing growth in government debt doesn't account for ongoing debt growth among companies, households, and students. None of these groups has been able to kick the debt habit.

So What's Wrong with Debt?

Broadly speaking, there are two types of debt: productive debt and unproductive debt. Borrowing to fund more consumption today is unproductive debt. Borrowing on your credit card to buy a big-screen TV falls into this category. It doesn't increase your productivity or sustainable income, and you are left with debt that eventually has to be funded by consuming less in the future. You have worsened your overall economic position. Not only have you shifted consumption from the future into the present, but you have decreased your overall potential consumption because you have to eventually pay for the cost of the TV *plus* the interest charged until the debt is paid off.

In contrast, productive debt allows you to fund an investment whose return exceeds the cost of the debt and which therefore improves your overall economic position. A farmer borrowing to buy more harvesters and increase his harvest can be productive. So can borrowing to pay for an education that significantly increases your future earning capacity. However, debt incurred for investment that is intended to be productive can end up being unproductive. Investments in productive assets like real estate can go bad if either the price paid for the asset or the interest rate turns out, in hindsight, to have been too high. The same holds true for student loans. Today, Americans are saddled with over $1.5 trillion[19] of student debt, much of which will end up being unproductive, because either (1) interest rates on this debt are too high, or (2) the price of the asset (in this case the cost of tuition) exceeds any benefit of increased earnings over time.

In the long run, productivity growth is what drives economic growth. Economic growth arises from political stability that supports property rights and consistent rule of law, because such stability encourages people to invest their surplus earnings in productive enterprises that generate economic profits. Productivity growth arises from advancements in technology and process know-how that facilitate the production of more goods and services *per unit* of capital and labor invested. These technological and process know-how improvements are often the result of the investment of surplus into profitable business activities. This is the virtuous cycle of productivity growth that gets set in motion by political stability, with one positive development leading to another in a self-reinforcing feedback loop. Provided that political stability can be maintained, productivity growth and accumulation of surplus can drive economic growth in perpetuity.

Productive debt, as defined above, can contribute to the overall productivity growth described above because a loan is somebody's asset (the lender's), and if the loan is productive, both borrower and lender end up wealthier. Sadly, it doesn't appear that most of the debt in the global economy is productive.

Promising unfunded Social Security and Medicare benefits so that millions of baby boomers can cease working at the age of 66 and live off the taxpayer for another 25 or more years in retirement is clearly unproductive. Leaving aside for the moment the ethical issues involved with this construct, it is an obvious case of nonproductive debt incurred for the sake of consuming more today.

Debt incurred to build new housing for productive workers should be a productive investment. But when interest rates are kept too low for too long, extreme misallocations of capital (which are destructive, not productive) can contribute to bubbles like the one in housing in the mid-2000s. Even after the popping of that bubble, we should question the existing system in which a buyer has to borrow over a million dollars to purchase a house in some American cities. That doesn't seem like a good way to encourage young couples to have kids who might drive the economic growth and tax base required to pay for government programs. And a trillion and a half dollars of student debt, much of it incurred to pay exorbitant tuition to colleges in order to achieve degrees that turn out to be of limited economic value, appears to be a vast misallocation of capital and therefore economically destructive, rather than productive.

Economist Hyman Minsky, who was largely unknown during his lifetime and died in 1996, became famous (at least in financial circles) after the Global Financial Crisis of 2008–2009. He had recognized the problem of borrowing to fund investments that are *hoped* to be productive, but *don't end up being* productive. Analyzing this problem in what he called the Financial Instability Hypothesis, he proposed a descriptive framework of three types of debt used to fund investments: (1) "hedge" debt, (2) "speculative" debt, and (3) "ponzi" debt.[20]

The first kind of debt, "hedge" debt, is sound and productive. A "hedge" debt borrower is someone (or some institution) who can pay the interest and principal from the current cash flow of the investment. A farmer who gets a five-year loan to finance the purchase of a harvester to reap more wheat and uses the profits generated from the larger crop to pay off the loan has incurred "hedge" debt.

The second kind of debt is riskier and more problematic. The "speculative" debt borrower counts on making a profit by reselling the asset he acquires at a higher price than he paid, but he's in trouble if he can't resell it at a profit because the cash flows from the asset only cover the interest payments and don't leave anything for repayment of the debt. An investor who buys an apartment building by taking out a mortgage and then collects rents that barely allow him to cover the mortgage payments and the maintenance expenses of the property has incurred "speculative debt." If the value of the apartment building does rise over time, he can refinance the loan when it comes due or sell the building to pay off the loan and realize an investment profit. But if the value of the apartment building falls over time, he ends up in the hole.

The third kind of debt, "ponzi" debt, is so problematic that it should never be incurred. Consider the real estate investor who gets an interest-only ARM (adjustable rate mortgage) in order to buy a house he intends to rent to some tenant. The ARM has a low fixed interest rate for the first five years, after which the rate will rise, while the rental income just barely covers the fixed mortgage payment during the low interest rate period, and won't cover it once the low interest rate period has ended. If the borrower isn't able to either refinance the loan or sell the property at a higher price than he paid, he will lose money. The value of the property has to rise just for the borrower to be able to repay the debt.

More Money, More Debt

Minsky and others before him recognized that debt also arises from central banks lowering interest rates and printing money. Indeed, debt expansion due to lower interest rates is one of the explicit aims of monetary policy. Central bankers reason that lower interest rates will induce people to borrow in order to fund entrepreneurial endeavors and expand existing businesses. They also figure that interest rates are the discount rate at which investors value their investments. If an investor can buy a government bond that yields 5% annually with very little default risk, then she might demand a 10% annual return from a stock since the stock investment entails more risk. Based on the fundamental financial model known as the "dividend discount model,"[21] demanding a 10% return implies that the stock will trade at a multiple of 100% / 10% = 10x cash flow, assuming no growth in cash flows over time. But if the government bond yields only 2%, then the investor might demand only a 5% annual return from a stock, which would imply 100% / 5% = 20x cash flow. This 20x cash flow valuation implies the stock doubling in price as compared to a 10x cash flow valuation implied by the 10% demanded return.

The same logic applies to real estate and other risk assets. Such increases in asset prices allow investors to take out more debt secured by those investments. Thus a business owner might seek to borrow money in order to grow her business more quickly since the interest rate is low, and the bank might be willing to lend her the money since in a lower interest rate environment, her business is worth more. Likewise, a homeowner might seek to take out a mortgage at a lower rate to improve her property, and the lender will be willing to lend since the property is worth more in the low interest rate environment.

Quantitative Queasing

In practice, the Federal Reserve effectively increases the amount of consumer, mortgage, and corporate debt via the "discount rate." The discount rate is the interest rate at which the banks borrow from the Fed.[22] By lowering the discount rate, the Federal Reserve reduces the banks' cost of funding and allows them to issue loans at lower interest rates. When loans are offered at lower interest rates, more consumers and businesses borrow, which increases the overall level of debt in the economy.

The Federal Reserve also increases the amount of debt in the economy by buying government bonds in the processes known as "open market operations" and "quantitative easing." It creates new money out of thin air to buy government debt, which reduces the average yield of that debt and reduces the interest rates on any new pieces of government debt that are benchmarked against the existing debt. Since the interest rates of all other forms of debt (corporate and consumer) are priced against government debt, this lowering of government debt yields/rates results in lower interest rates for all types of debt across the economy. Again, lower-cost debt causes people and businesses to borrow more.

Additionally, the reduction in interest rates on government debt allows the government to fund greater budget deficits by reducing the interest burden associated with the incremental debt. $20 trillion of government debt at an average interest rate of 3% is no worse than $10 trillion of government debt at an average interest rate of 6%, provided that lenders are willing to hold the incremental debt because they believe they'll be repaid their principal and interest without significant capital loss due to inflation. But there is undoubtedly a limit to how much debt a government can incur before its lenders refuse to lend more.

If the dramatic rise in debt in the United States and across the world had been of the productive type rather than the unproductive, consumption-driven variety, we would expect to see an increase in economic growth. More specifically, we would expect to see an acceleration in economic growth subsequent to the incurrence of the debt, and such acceleration would be expected to result in the economy growing more rapidly than the debt burden. This would result in a decrease in the ratio of debt to GDP. Instead, we observe the opposite: a dramatic rise in the ratio of debt to GDP. The only thing that has kept the interest expense of this debt from crushing borrowers has been the inexorable fall in interest rates due to policies of central banks such as the Federal Reserve.

John Kenneth Galbraith is one of the great thinkers on financial economics and specifically financial bubbles. In *The Great Crash, 1929*, he wrote about a concept he called "the bezzle." [23] Economist John Kay later summarized "the bezzle" as "that increment to wealth that occurs during the magic interval when a confidence trickster knows he has the money he has appropriated but the victim does not yet understand that he has lost it." [24] When the perpetrator of a fraud knows he has the money but his victim still thinks he has the money, the same dollar gets counted twice. Cases such as Bernie Madoff, and many before him, including the great Charles Ponzi (who lent his name to Minsky's "ponzi" debt category), illustrate the concept. Schemes such as these are either fraudulent from the outset, or from the point in time at which the scheme ceases to be able to support all the claims of the investors.

Today there is a much larger bezzle. We call it government debt. Our own governments (federal, state, and local) know they cannot satisfy the debt claims that citizens have on them. As noted earlier, in the United States the accumulated liabilities, including outstanding debt and unfunded Social Security and Medicare, exceed $210 trillion in addition to the growing commercial and consumer debts. Those claims are legal, but they are unpayable. Not only can the economy not support the principal owed, but the interest cost alone is unserviceable at interest rates above the rock-bottom ones that prevail today. I don't know when or how it will end. But I do have high confidence in one conclusion. The greater the accumulated debt when the unwind occurs, the more devastating the unwind will be. So, as with a heroin addict, we must do our best to get him off the junk before he overdoses.

While the addict's plight is tragic, it might be argued that at least there is some level of self-infliction. In contrast, the cost of the debt problem, including the unfunded pension and healthcare programs, won't be borne by those who incurred it. It will be borne by later generations who neither benefited from this massive wealth transfer nor voted in favor of it. So how did the world get up to its eyeballs in what is essentially a ponzi debt that will be owed by future generations? A full treatment of this topic is too lengthy for this book, but I will invoke a few anecdotes from my own professional experience to illustrate some of the causes.

Inside Job

One year into my job at the "reputable" Wall Street firm mentioned in Chapter 1, I received a recruiting call from an even more reputable Wall Street firm. The economic wreckage of the bursting of the dotcom bubble and the September 11 terrorist attacks was clearing, and the firm was short of staff. A few weeks later, in November 2004, I was working at Goldman Sachs.

The mid-2000s were high times for Goldman. Led by career investment banker Henry "Hank" Paulson, Goldman reported record profits in those years between the end of the dotcom bubble and the Global Financial Crisis of 2008–2009. Although I was an inexperienced analyst near the bottom of the pecking order of front-office professionals, I did gain a modest amount of exposure to some of the firm's upper echelon. At the time, I was told that approximately 2% of Goldman's employees held the title of "Partner." The average annual compensation of these folks was rumored to be around $8 million in 2004 when I joined the firm. Aside from their generous pay packages, the thing that stood out about the Partners was how they spent their time, most of which seemed to be devoted to managing conflicts of interest.

In hindsight, it's obvious why the Partners spent so much time managing conflicts of interest. It's because their job wasn't just to make money—their job was to extract *every last dollar out of every deal that came across their desks*. That didn't just mean representing one party to a transaction or making an investment on behalf of a single client or on behalf of the firm's own balance sheet. It meant trying to get a piece of every possible angle of every single situation. Soon after I joined the firm, one of my bosses noted that he had been working on a deal that was known as a "triple play." This meant that Goldman was involved on three sides of the deal. But he noted that we would soon be working on a "quadruple play." His excitement was palpable.

In 2005 a company called MeadWestVaco signed a deal to sell its paper business to a private equity fund called Cerberus.[25] Named for the three-headed dog in Greek mythology that guards the gates of the underworld to prevent the dead from escaping, Cerberus won the deal by beating other bidders for the assets. My recollection is that one of those bidders was Goldman's own private equity department. Goldman also advised Cerberus on the acquisition. For this service Goldman received a multimillion-dollar advisory fee. My team, which was responsible for arranging financing for heavily indebted companies (an endeavor known as "leveraged finance") provided debt for the deal in exchange for a multimillion-dollar fee. In addition, Goldman provided a complex hedging contract to the company to mitigate the risk of price movements in the commodity inputs to its manufacturing process. For this service, my friend on the commodities hedging desk told me at the time that Goldman had booked a $50 million profit. My recollection is that, in total, Goldman managed to earn something on the order of $100 million in fees for the various services it provided, all while competing with its own client to acquire the target. Not bad for a single transaction!

Three years later, in May 2008, Goldman helped NewPage (the successor company to MeadWestVaco) file for an IPO. A few months later Goldman's mezzanine debt fund lent the company $2.1 billion, and another Goldman fund (GS Credit Partners) lent the company additional money in the form of a senior secured term loan and revolving credit facility (which is basically a credit line).[26] Three years after that in 2011, NewPage filed for bankruptcy. Goldman ended up owning the company. Playing multiple sides of a deal? What could possibly go wrong?

When I completed my analyst program at Goldman in 2006 and moved to an independent private equity investment fund, it would still be another year and a half until the bankruptcy filing of Lehman Brothers, which triggered the Global Financial Crisis of 2008–2009 that brought the global economy to its knees. Only after that disaster would I realize the true extent of all the angles that Goldman was playing.

By that time, Goldman's CEO, Hank Paulson, had moved on. He had secured an appointment as U.S. Treasury Secretary, arguably the second most powerful financial official in the nation (behind the Federal Reserve Chairman). Paulson and others orchestrated the biggest government bailout of private industry in the history of the world. By helping to organize the (1) pumping of billions of cash dollars directly into the banks, and (2) granting of government guarantees to save AIG, he directly funded the livelihoods of his former colleagues, as well as Goldman's shareholders.

The AIG case was the most egregious. Goldman had been more clever than its competitors and had taken steps to hedge the firm against the risk of the housing market collapsing. It had entered billions of dollars' worth of credit default swap (CDS) contracts that would pay off in the event of a housing crisis. This would act as a hedge against the potential losses that a housing meltdown could inflict on Goldman's overall balance sheet. Unfortunately for Goldman, the primary counterparty to those contracts, which would have to pay up to fund these hedges, was a single company: AIG. Goldman had acquired CDS contracts with AIG with notional values of $21 billion.[27] AIG had effectively written insurance contracts on housing with payout values that amounted to multiples of its own equity capital. It was ludicrously undercapitalized and had the ability to pay out only a small fraction of the claims it had written. Goldman had enough debt on its own balance sheet that if AIG were to fail, so would Goldman. So in coordination with the Federal Reserve, ex-Goldman-CEO Paulson and others made sure that the full faith and credit of the U.S. government saved AIG, which resulted in saving Goldman.

A year after the Global Financial Crisis of 2008–2009, it emerged that Goldman had done things in addition to pulling government strings to get AIG bailed out. Goldman's structured credit department, which dealt in the mortgage-backed securities that were at the center of the crisis, went so far as to allow one of the firm's clients (hedge fund Paulson & Co.—no relation to

Hank Paulson) to specifically hand-pick securities that Goldman expected to default and create a portfolio of such securities. Then, Goldman told investors on the opposite side of the transaction that the portfolio of doomed securities had been selected by an independent, objective third party. Goldman ultimately paid $550 million to settle the ensuing fraud case brought by the SEC.[28]

The greatest tragedy of the Global Financial Crisis of 2008–2009 wasn't that none of the senior executives at the big banks went to jail. It wasn't that numerous bank executives earned and kept tens of millions of dollars of annual compensation by piling on risk that contributed directly to the crisis. It wasn't even that millions of Americans lost their jobs or their homes in the deep recession and housing crisis. No, the greatest tragedy was that most of the underlying problems in the system were never fixed.

At the time of the crisis, all the biggest banks were "too big to fail." One of them (Lehman Brothers) did fail, and it almost brought down the entire system. Today the biggest bank in the United States (JP Morgan) has a balance sheet that is far larger than that of the biggest bank just prior to the crisis. The same is true in other parts of the world. Banks have continued to merge and grow, and despite the fact that their balance sheets are less leveraged than before the crisis (at its peak, Lehman's liabilities were roughly 40x its equity[29]), the big banks have grown so much that they are each now far too big to fail. This means that their risk of insolvency is fully borne by taxpayers like you and me. Wall Street has managed to fully institutionalize its ability to reap private gains while pushing the risk of losses onto taxpayers and ordinary citizens. Heads, they win. Tails, we lose. What a racket. I'm not proud to have been employed for three years in this industry.

While Goldman's activities adequately illustrate the system's ongoing failures, other banks make Goldman's misdeeds look modest in comparison. In the decade after the Global Financial Crisis, American and European banks illegally foreclosed on homeowners,[30] manipulated Libor[31] (the basis for *trillions* of dollars' worth of financial contracts, making it one of the world's most important financial statistics), manipulated commodity markets,[32] rigged multiple foreign currency exchange rates,[33] opened millions of unauthorized customer accounts,[34] and laundered hundreds of billions of criminal funds,[35] among other misdeeds. After paying *over $300 billion* of fines and penalties in the decade ending in 2017,[36] the banks have joined the pantheon of the most crooked industries on the planet. It's not an exaggeration to describe the recent story of the banking industry in the words of journalist Matt Taibbi as "not an economic story, but a crime story."[37] It's worth wondering why we tolerate such a level of criminality in one of the most important industries in our economy.

The Revolving Door of Merry Banksters

Hank Paulson's neat trick of becoming fabulously rich as CEO of Goldman, while his company defrauded some of his own clients and created instability in the financial system, is not unique. Far from it—it has been pulled off by numerous people on Wall Street. Prior to Paulson, the textbook case was that of Robert "Bob" Rubin, who completed the full 360-degree rotation through the "revolving door" from Wall Street to government and back again. Rubin spent 26 years at Goldman, rising to co-CEO and co-Chairman before becoming Treasury Secretary for President Bill Clinton. Then in 1999 he joined Citigroup as a board member and strategic advisor.[38] In the ensuing decade he received over $125 million in compensation. As soon as the Global Financial Crisis hit (still on Rubin's watch), Citigroup became insolvent and was bailed out with the rest of the major banks.[39] As far as I know, Rubin kept his compensation.

In his brilliant book *Skin in the Game,* Nassim Taleb argues that the "revolving door" only malfunctions in one direction—from government to the private sector. The obvious problem with government employees moving into management positions on Wall Street is that the banks can reward civil servants who serve the banks' interests with lucrative pay packages after they leave government and avoid hiring civil servants who don't serve their interests. It doesn't take too many recruiting cycles for civil servants to see the pattern and become bank-friendly in order to get hired by a bank and cash some big checks after a career in government. However, Taleb argues that the reverse scenario of a finance professional achieving success in the private sector and ending his career in government is harmless because the individual has already made his money beforehand rather than using his seat of power as a tool to subsequently cash in.

But this perspective ignores the issue of Wall Streeters moving into government and using their newfound power to protect their friends and cronies, as Hank Paulson did when orchestrating the bailouts that saved Goldman. It also ignores a unique financial opportunity afforded to executives who transition from Wall Street to government. It turns out that Paulson didn't even have to save Goldman to maintain his personal wealth because although he held hundreds of millions of dollars' worth of Goldman stock when he left the firm, section 1043 of the Internal Revenue Code allowed him to sell all of his stock and reinvest the proceeds in other assets *without paying capital gains tax*.[40] This provision of the tax code, which applies only to employees of the Executive Branch, is intended to "minimize the burden of government service" resulting from forced divestiture. So Paulson personally made hundreds of millions (and possibly more than $1 billion) while his firm defrauded some of its clients and actively helped to blow up the financial system, and he didn't even have to pay capital gains tax! In a world in which the banking industry has captured its regulators, it turns out that the merry banksters can have the taxpayers' cake and eat it too.

Chapter 4

The Bigger Picture

Still Broken

The Global Financial Crisis of 2008–2009 was an extreme event. It could not have happened without a confluence of causes, a concept that legendary investor and Warren Buffett partner Charlie Munger calls a "lollapalooza effect."[41] The list of major causes of the crises includes: (1) mortgage lenders skipping on paperwork and procedures to help borrowers take on mortgages they couldn't afford, (2) borrowers willingly lying about their creditworthiness, (3) government policy (via Department of Housing and Urban Development and others) encouraging banks to lend to help people buy houses they couldn't afford, (4) Congress repealing Glass-Steagall to allow investment banks to mix more staid commercial banking with risky investment banking, (5) banks being allowed to incur enough leverage and grow large enough to become "too big to fail," (6) banks getting "creative" and repackaging credit instruments and selling them to gullible investors without banks retaining much of the risk on their own balance sheets, (7) risk managers and credit rating agencies failing to use realistic models of distress for financial markets, (8) lack of transparency about banks' and other financial institutions' exposure to each other via derivatives like credit default swaps (CDS), (9) the Federal Reserve keeping interest rates too low for too long, and (10) the growth of the offshore dollar liability ("Eurodollar") market, resulting in a shortage of dollars for desperate borrowers with short-term dollar liabilities. This list is not exhaustive, and the details have been ably chronicled in numerous other books, including Andrew Ross Sorkin's comprehensive tome *Too Big to Fail*.

The aforementioned Hyman Minsky knew that periods of stability foster ever-greater risk taking, which leads to crisis if not contained (via the Financial Instability Hypothesis referenced earlier). Given that the world had been off a gold-based standard for 37 years, and debt levels rose inexorably through that period, it isn't so shocking that we ended up with the Global Financial Crisis in 2008–2009. What is shocking is that we didn't fix the underlying problems in order to prevent it from happening again!

Glass-Steagall (the law that separated commercial banking from investment banking) has *not* been reinstated. The banks are even larger (much larger, in fact) than they used to be, and there are now more of them that are too big to fail. Financial derivatives markets are still gigantic. And the banks have continued to flout the law at the expense of their customers and taxpayers. Most importantly, the Federal Reserve has kept interest rates so low for so long that the total quantity of debt in the economy has not fallen significantly from its peak, and it remains over 325% of GDP (not including the much larger unfunded Social Security and Medicare benefits).

I don't believe this could have happened without the revolving door of bank executives through government, and I don't believe it will be fixed until that problem of "regulatory capture" (industry controlling the regulators instead of the reverse) is solved. I don't see any signs that it will be.

Marx, Engels, and Keynes; Stalin, Mao, and Greenspan

History is full of politicians and policymakers who justify government policies by invoking political and economic theorists. They often act with good intent. Unfortunately for their citizens, the theories they put into practice often have disastrous results. We need look no further than Karl Marx and Friedrich Engels to see those results.

Marx and Engels promulgated some insightful concepts in *The Communist Manifesto*. They shed light on the struggle between economic classes, including between the laborers who do the work and the owners of capital who control the means of production. Vladimir Lenin invoked Marx and Engels' ideas in the creation of the centralized economic system of what would become the Stalinist Soviet Union. Admitting that history is complicated, and that Lenin's and Stalin's interpretation and implementation of those ideas were flawed, it still seems fair to say that in its deployment of communist theory, the Soviet Union managed to cause immense suffering and death to large portions of its own population and those of its neighbors, while also threatening to destroy human civilization in possible nuclear war with the United States. Likewise, tens of millions of Chinese suffered grievously under Mao's disastrous Great Leap Forward and Cultural Revolution, which were partly based on Mao's interpretation of Marx and Engels. All told, historians estimate that communism in the Soviet Union and China directly caused the deaths of tens of millions of people.

When I ask people why they think communism failed, they usually tell me you don't get significant economic growth without capitalism because capitalism is the only way to motivate entrepreneurs to start and grow businesses that grow the overall economy. I don't doubt that's a major factor. It's hard to imagine high levels of innovation without a large chunk of the resulting economic benefits flowing directly to the innovators themselves.

But there is a bigger problem with communism: it eliminates the price signal, which is the very heart of economics. Without a system in which consumers and producers meet freely in a market to discover the clearing price of a good, suppliers will have no idea what goods to produce or in what quantity. Ludwig von Mises and Friedrich Hayek, two giants of the Austrian school of economics, highlight the importance of the price signal in works such as *Socialism* (Mises 1922)[42] and *The Use of Knowledge in Society* (Hayek 1945).[43] They argue that in a complex economy (which describes the modern world), it is impossible for any individual or group to gain the expertise required for an efficient allocation of all products and services traded in such an economy. On the supply side (the side of the economy that produces useful stuff), such an all-knowing person or group would have to develop deep expertise in the design, manufacturing processes, and supply chain dynamics of every single product and service produced in the economy. In reality, it takes a diligent and intelligent manager of a business decades of experience to master the production of *just a single good or service*. Yet in order for a centrally planned economy to succeed, there has to be someone or something—a person, a centralized group of government bureaucrats, a software algorithm—capable of applying that kind of expertise to the production processes of all goods and services in the economy, and of being able to assess the aggregate demand for those products and services, including which consumers might use them, how they would be used, and in what quantities. Mises recognized that communism was destined to fail because no planned economy could complete such economic calculations.

Before Mises and Hayek diagnosed this problem, Adam Smith had identified the solution: the "invisible hand" of the marketplace, which uses the price signal to match buyers and sellers, and also drives entrepreneurs and investors to allocate their time and their capital in such a way as to optimize the production and provision of goods and services in order to meet consumers' demands.[44] It is the trial and error of independent entrepreneurs, backed by investors motivated by a desire for profits, that drives innovation and also allocates more capital to those goods and services demanded by consumers. As Mises articulated in *Human Action*, the consumer signals her preferences with her pocketbook, and the entrepreneurial capitalist finds a way to efficiently meet her demand. The surplus created in the process, which accrues partly to the consumer and partly to the producer, enriches society. Any society that lacks the price signal that enables this highly productive system is doomed to poverty.

There is perhaps no better modern example of the critical role of the price signal than China's rapid economic rise. More people have risen out of poverty and into the middle class in China than in any other country in history. This rapid transformation did not occur by accident. After Mao's disastrous policies in the 1950s and 1960s, Deng Xiaoping recognized the importance of the price signal and realized that private enterprise was China's best (and possibly only) route to development. China's transition toward capitalism began in the late 1970s with Deng's economic reforms. Having largely completed the transition, China is now a single-party autocracy that allows a significant level of capitalism in order to drive economic growth. Its government is top-down and highly centralized, but much of its economy operates on the principles of the free market. Whether China can innovate at the level of *democratic* capitalist societies like the United States remains to be seen. But there is little doubt that China has achieved significant economic growth, and that a portion of that growth has been caused by innovative entrepreneurial enterprise driven by both self-interest and price signals.

If Marx and Engels brought us Stalin and Mao, then John Maynard Keynes brought us Alan Greenspan, who served as Chairman of the Federal Reserve from 1987 to 2006. In stark contrast to the economists of the Austrian school, Keynes promulgated the theory that central banks and governments could smooth out the peaks and valleys of the business cycle by actively managing the economy at a macro level.[45] An economic downturn could be mitigated by increasing government spending (fiscal stimulus) and increasing the money supply (monetary stimulus). Once the economy was back on its feet, the fiscal and monetary stimulus could be removed. Unfortunately, as with communism, the devil is in the details, including the mechanisms and the incentives of those wielding power.

The major problem with fiscal stimulus is painfully obvious. Politicians set budgets. Since they are elected on two-year, four-year or six-year cycles, they have to deliver economic goodies to their voters in real time. And as long as bond markets will support the growing liabilities accrued with deficit spending, the temptation to promise short-term economic benefits to voters is too great. A member of Congress who fails to deliver the fiscal goods to voters now is unlikely to see another term in office. This "pork barrel" problem is well known, and considering the incentives, it's no surprise that politicians are willing to mortgage the future in order to feed their constituents today. While Democrats and Republicans differ in their approach to deficit spending—Democrats prefer to increase spending on social programs, while Republicans cut taxes and increase military spending—both parties have agreed on the expediency of the government spending more than it collects in taxes.

The political power of the baby boomer generation, which has managed to dominate politics for decades, suck financial benefits out of the system, and leave the younger generations with the bill, has exacerbated the problem. Since one of the reasons I wrote this book was to educate my clients and family members, and since quite a few of my clients and family members are baby boomers, there is a reasonable chance that you, dear reader, are in this cohort. I hope you don't take personal offense at my characterization of the situation. The vast majority of baby boomers I know are wonderful, ethical, kind, loving people, and that probably includes you. Moreover, I suspect that a large portion of the baby boomer generation isn't aware of the scale of the wealth it has transferred from younger generations to itself.

One of the most significant future political conflicts I foresee is that between the younger generations and the older ones. While such tension has existed in all societies, the scale of the wealth transfer in this case will likely raise this conflict to a higher magnitude if left unsolved. I can envision a narrative in which the Generation X and Millennial generations come to think of the older generations like their dinner partner who inconveniently goes to the bathroom right before the check arrives.

If ever-increasing fiscal stimulus (deficit spending) were occurring in isolation without the help of monetary stimulus, the problem might find itself contained by the bond market. Investors in government debt (who lend to the government through their purchases of bonds) would demand higher interest rates to compensate for the risk that deficit spending might result in the government's reduced ability to repay the debt. The cost of borrowing money due to higher interest rates would impose fiscal rectitude and decrease reckless spending sooner rather than later. But budget-busting politicians have had a willing and able partner supporting their spending habits: The Federal Reserve under Alan Greenspan, Ben Bernanke, Janet Yellen, and Jay Powell.

Inflation Nowhere and Everywhere

When I took Econ 101, the textbook presented a concept called the Phillips Curve. Named for William Phillips, who might have garnered a Nobel Prize in Economics had he lived past the age of 60, the Phillips curve is still one of the key pillars of economics as it is taught today. The Phillips Curve simply plots on a graph the relationship between unemployment and consumer price inflation. This concept is the "North Star" of the Federal Reserve, the world's most powerful central bank. In 1977 (six years after Nixon severed the dollar's official link to gold) Congress tasked the Federal Reserve with two jobs. This "dual mandate" comprises (1) keeping people employed, and (2) keeping prices stable.[46]

These are laudable goals. But keeping prices stable has come to be defined narrowly as keeping prices of *goods and services* stable. Let's return to the three classifications of goods from Chapter 2: (1) consumption goods, (2) capital goods, and (3) money. Your Econ 101 textbook will explain how you get "inflation" in the prices of consumption goods. Such inflation in "consumer prices" is popularly measured in the "consumer price index" (CPI), though central bankers have other similar metrics for it, such as "personal consumption expenditures" (PCE).[47]

However it is measured, the inflation is believed to occur via the "wage-price spiral." The mechanism is simple. The central bank prints money via channels discussed earlier. Consumers take the incremental new money and they feel richer. So they save some of it, but they also spend some of it. This increase in overall spending (also known as an increase in "aggregate demand") means they buy more consumption goods. This causes the companies that make those goods to raise production since they see an opportunity to increase their revenue and profits. But in order to make more goods, they have to find more labor. At the margin, securing more labor means either (1) paying existing workers to work more hours, or (2) enticing non-workers to join the workforce. Either way, convincing existing or prospective workers to toil more hours per week than they did before requires raising their wages. Raising workers' wages puts more money in their pockets, which causes them to demand more goods. A self-reinforcing feedback loop results in rising wages and consumer goods prices.

This logic seems sound, but the economy is more complex. There are at least two other major factors at work: (1) trade, and (2) technology. With the exception of the last few years, the last several decades were a period of increasing international trade in which greater volumes of goods and services were traded across national borders. But the growth in international trade really kicked into high gear when China joined the World Trade Organization (WTO) in December of 2001.[48] China's effect on world trade is evident in Figure 2.

Figure 2: World Exports

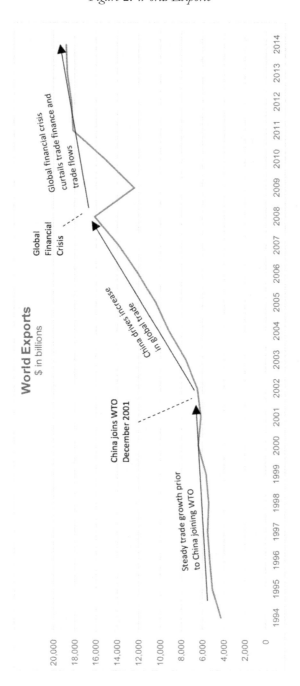

Data source: International Monetary Fund, https://imf.org/en Data; text source: Andy Edstrom

Instead of paying high wages to American workers, some of whom were unionized, companies built factories in China to take advantage of much cheaper labor there. These new factories increased demand for Chinese workers, and in the 2002–2014 period, Chinese manufacturing wages roughly *quadrupled* as a result.[49] Meanwhile, as Chinese employment and wages increased, large portions of the American manufacturing labor force lost their jobs or saw their wages stagnate. The wage-price spiral described earlier broke down because instead of demand for manufactured goods driving up wages—and therefore prices—in the United States, those wage gains occurred overseas, and manufactured goods actually became cheaper over time in the United States. These goods experienced price *deflation*, rather than inflation.

Meanwhile, another factor appears to have kept American wages and prices of manufactured goods low: automation technology. One of the great benefits of technology is that it reduces the cost of production over time by (1) automating greater portions of the production process to reduce the labor costs, and (2) allowing the discovery and implementation of processes that result in greater efficiencies in non-labor inputs, including materials and energy. More efficient processes are used over time, and a portion of the reduced production costs is passed on to the consumer in the form of lower prices. Globalized international trade with supply chains originating in low-labor-cost Asian countries, coupled with efficiency gains from technology, kept the prices of consumption goods in the United States and other wealthy countries from rising much over the last few decades, and in many cases reduced them.

Thus the combined effects of technological efficiencies and the offshoring of manufacturing have joined to keep overall consumer price inflation low, even as interest rates in the U.S. have continued to fall. The numbered statements in Figure 3 trace the history of the interaction between interest rates, consumer prices, and inflation/deflation. (1) When the U.S. left the Bretton Woods gold standard, consumer price inflation was around 5% annually. (2) Inflation spiked in the late 1970s as OPEC restricted the supply of oil, then the life blood of the U.S. economy, and the price of oil skyrocketed. (3) After Paul Volcker became Chairman of the Federal Reserve Board in 1979, the Federal Reserve responded by raising interest rates in order to drive consumer price inflation back downward. (4) But for a short time, the wage/price feedback loop remained strong enough that consumer price inflation continued to rise. (5) Then, after a relatively brief period of time, the Fed's high-interest-rate policy proved successful and inflation fell. (6) In the subsequent decades, successive Federal Reserve bankers lowered rates through business cycles, which in normal circumstances would result in higher prices, yet the inflationary effects of the wage/price feedback loop appear to have been outweighed by the deflationary effects of automation and trade discussed earlier.

While the price of the overall consumer goods basket was kept low due to *deflation* in prices of manufactured goods, it is instructive to look at those "consumer goods" whose prices *were not* kept low and instead inflated significantly in recent decades. The categories that stand out are (1) healthcare, (2) housing, and (3) education.

In the United States, healthcare has been a uniquely dysfunctional market for several reasons. First, doctors have to mitigate their own financial liability both by carrying expensive insurance and also prescribing excessive levels of diagnostic tests. Second, consumers (patients) usually have no idea of the price of services they are consuming and usually aren't directly paying for them anyway so have no incentive to avoid overspending. Third, healthcare providers are often incentivized to provide tests and treatments whether or not they are needed since they make more money the more services they dispense.

These problems have been somewhat mitigated over time due to tort reform, improvements to government-payer healthcare (Medicare and Affordable Care Act, a.k.a. "Obamacare"), and the rise of managed care. The latter system gives the healthcare provider an incentive to deliver better health results rather than just order more tests, procedures, and treatments. Nevertheless, we are still mostly stuck with the extraordinary expense of care for very sick and near-death patients (who generally don't pay for their own care), rapid technological advancement that increases the availability of very expensive treatments (again, not usually paid for by the recipient), and the fact that much of the innovation happens in the U.S. but is copied at lower cost elsewhere without fully compensating those who pay for the care in the U.S.

Figure 3: Consumer Price Inflation and 10-Year Government Bond Yields

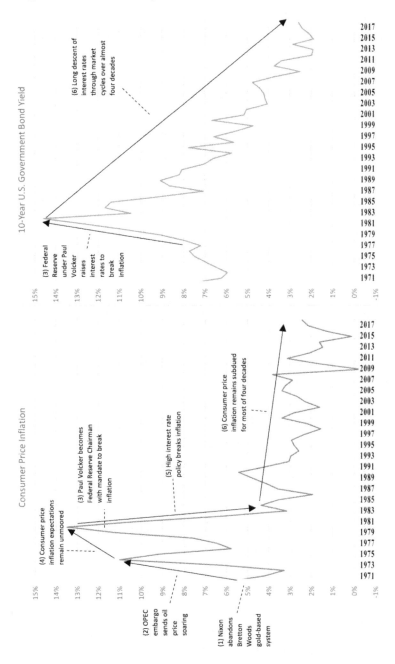

The net outcome has been costs rising so rapidly that healthcare now accounts for approximately 18% of the total GDP in the United States.[50,51] This means the U.S. spends more than double the average of the 36 countries in the OECD (the Organization for Economic Co-operation and Development—a club of 36 mostly rich nations). And what do we get for our money? The average American dies 1.7 years earlier than the average OECD citizen. This longevity gap has grown by a year since 2003.[52] Because of its unique structure, we will leave our analysis of the U.S. healthcare market at that and proceed to the other two major high-inflation categories (housing and education), because they shed light on some of the broader problems with the financial system that Bitcoin helps to redress.

As discussed in Chapter 2, housing is both a basic consumption good, since people consume shelter, and a capital good, since it is based on real estate, which is a long-lived productive asset. In the United States, roughly 65% of households own their own homes,[53] and 63% of those have mortgages.[54] Since mortgage debt is on average the single largest input to the overall cost of housing, the Fed's habit of money printing and lowering of interest rates has allowed home buyers to take on larger amounts of mortgage debt to bid up the prices of houses, especially in metro areas with strong economies and limitations on construction of new housing.

One of the more bizarre and disingenuous phenomena in the U.S. government's reporting of inflation data is the way it treats housing costs. In 2018 housing costs accounted for 42.2% of the Consumer Price Index, making it by far the largest category.[55] This makes housing by far the largest component of the household budget. And prices for this largest component of the household budget have reached record levels.[56] Working adults in their 20s and 30s commonly complain that they can't afford the down payment on a house. These complaints are justified. Data from the Bureau of Labor Statistics, one of the U.S. government's key sources for economic data, reported that in the 2000–2018 period the *cost of housing* (measured by the urban consumer price index) rose by 2.46% annually.[57] But in the same period the Case-Schiller U.S. National Home Price Index—probably the most-followed index of home prices in the U.S.—indicates that urban *house prices* rose by 3.88% annually.[58] This is a big difference. Thanks to compounding, the cumulative difference between these two figures is huge, with urban "housing costs" rising 59% in that eighteen-year period, and urban "house prices" rising 105%. In other words, house prices rose almost twice as much as housing costs!

You might think that *house prices* and *housing costs* are the same. The U.S. government disagrees. The reason for the discrepancy between 59% and 105% is that in 1983 the Bureau of Labor Statistics stopped using actual home prices to measure the housing cost component of the Consumer Price Index. Instead it started using a figure called "owners' equivalent rent of residences," which is their estimate of how much rent the homeowner's house would generate if the homeowner were renting it.[59] Effectively, the reported "inflation" of this living cost is the Bureau's estimate of how much the homeowner raises the rent on herself each year.

In one respect, this method is logical. As noted in Chapter 1, housing is part capital good and part consumption good. And if you keep lowering interest rates, then the total cost of ownership is reduced (all else being equal), which means that landlords don't have to raise rents as quickly as home prices rise. So lowering interest rates does help contain the housing component of living cost *provided you don't mind being priced out of the opportunity to own a house.* I imagine having the following conversation with my brother, who is in his early 30s.

Me: Great news, brother! Low interest rates have helped reduce your housing cost of living.

My Brother: Yeah, but I don't want to rent for the rest of my life. I want to buy my own house so I can raise a family.

Me: Oh, no problem, bro. Mortgage rates are lower so you can afford the same mortgage payment as people did thirty years ago when houses were much cheaper.

My Brother: Yeah, but those low interest rates have raised home prices so rapidly that now I have to scrape together $200,000 of cash just for the 20% down payment on a starter house in a major U.S. city. Despite being a doctor with higher income than most people my age, it would still take me years to accumulate that down payment. And that's if I weren't saddled with student loans!

Me: Hmm, good point. Well, at least you'll be well provided for in retirement by our great country's fully-funded Social Security and Medicare programs!

- AWKWARD SILENCE -

Although the public seems to pay more attention to CPI, the Federal Reserve claims to be more focused on another inflation index known as Personal Consumption Expenditures (PCE).[60] This is another inflation measure. PCE's housing cost component is roughly fifteen percentage points lower than CPI's, and the attendant owners' equivalent rent component is roughly ten percentage points lower than CPI's. Nevertheless, it still accounts for a large component of the index. Anyway, the Federal Reserve admits that it "closely tracks other inflation measures as well, including the consumer price indexes and producer price indexes issued by the Department of Labor." Such indices produced by the Department of Labor undoubtedly include the CPI, which is produced by the Bureau of Labor Statistics, as mentioned earlier.

Now let's look at what's happened to the cost of a college degree. Education is a capital good even more than housing is. Rather than being consumed just for survival or entertainment, most education is an investment in human capital with the expectation that it will help the student earn higher wages in the future. Today, student debt in the United States exceeds $1.5 trillion[61] and is widely considered one of the biggest problems facing young adults. As with housing, the printing of money and lowering of interest rates have fostered the creation of this debt, and the availability of it has allowed universities to raise tuition prices as students compete to pay up for scarce spots. This is the same dynamic described earlier in which lower interest rates allow people to bid up the prices of houses.

Not only are students being saddled with immense amounts of debt, but many students who had leaned on cheap loans and government debt support don't even graduate. This is particularly a problem for those who attend for-profit colleges. The six-year graduation rate for full-time students in the 2010–2016 period was a dismal *26%* at for-profit institutions, versus 66% at non-profit institutions.[62] And that's not the worst of it. Many students who *are* lucky enough to graduate will find that the degrees they acquired are not marketable.

What we see happening with housing and education costs highlights a major problem with monetary policy. Because these goods are frequently financed with debt, and because the Federal Reserve has pushed interest rates lower and lower over decades, the prices of these debt-financed goods have been driven ever-upward over time.

Let's return to our three classifications of goods from Chapter 2: (1) consumption goods, (2) capital goods, and (3) money. When the Federal Reserve creates more money, this money has to flow somewhere, assuming people don't hoard all of it. It might have manifested in rising prices for consumption goods if the effects of international trade, which resulted in a loss of jobs to China (and other cheap-labor countries), combined with improvements in technology, hadn't had the opposite effect, resulting in a lowering of the prices of consumption goods. Instead this money appears to have flowed into (1) capital goods, and (2) consumption goods that behave like capital goods (housing and education).

The Federal Reserve and other central banks across the developed world have made it clear that containing "inflation" in the prices of *capital* goods (and the associated asset price bubbles) is strictly outside their purview. We are left in a situation in which central bankers tell us "Look, consumer price inflation is so low and has been for decades. We are doing such a great job." Yet we've seen the prices of investment assets (capital goods) rise to ever-higher multiples of the cash flows that they generate and huge asset bubbles—most notably the housing bubble of the early-mid 2000s—inflate and pop, all while global debt continues its seemingly inexorable rise. It's a bit like when the child with toys and clothes strewn across the floor of his bedroom sweeps them all into the closet, closes the door, and proudly declares "Mom, my room is clean." Most of the "mess" of inflation has been pushed into capital goods, which includes housing and education.

For the economy at large there are serious consequences for the inflation of capital goods. And at the individual level it can be disastrous. In Chapter 1 we noted that the first instrument to solve the "coincidence of wants" problem in primitive economies was probably personal debt. But once the economy scales up and takes advantage of specialization, such a system of incurring and settling debts for consumer goods is inefficient. The reason the nice lady selling brussels sprouts at the farmer's market won't just hand them to me in exchange for a promise to pay her later is that she might not ever see me again. The cost to her of collecting on the debt will therefore exceed the value of the debt.

For much larger transactions, however, such as those for capital goods, which tend to be high-ticket items, the effort of collecting on a debt is justified. In the case of housing, for example, if I stop making payments on my house, it is well worth the lender's time, effort, and expense, to foreclose on my house. In the case of an education loan, since personal bankruptcy laws won't allow me to rid myself of this kind of debt, I am doomed to repay the loan, even if the education I incurred the debt for doesn't increase my earnings. If the lender is tenacious enough, he can garnish my wages in order to repay the debt!

To the Rich Even Greater Spoils

Once we realize that the Federal Reserve and other central banks have been pumping tons of money into capital goods, it's no surprise that we are reaching record levels of wealth inequality, with the top 0.1% of the U.S. population owning almost as much wealth as the bottom 90%.[63] Ask your cleaning lady how her stock portfolio is doing these days. You might be met with a blank stare. The less-wealthy segments of the population don't have investments. They don't have significant assets in 401(k)s, and they are much more likely to rent than own their homes. They don't benefit from ever-falling interest rates that cause ever-rising stock and real estate prices. Printing money and lowering interest rates props up asset prices, which directly exacerbates the disparity in wealth between the very rich and the rest by further enriching those who already own assets.

The effect of this subsidy to those who already own investment assets appears to be substantial. A paper published by Mehdi El Herradi and Aurélien Leroy of the central bank of the Netherlands concludes the following: "The results obtained from both empirical methods indicate that loose monetary conditions strongly increase the top one percent's income and vice versa. In fact, following an expansionary monetary policy shock, the share of national income held by the richest 1 percent increases by approximately 1 to 6 percentage points."[64]

In 2013 a relatively unknown French economist named Thomas Piketty published *Capital in the Twenty-First Century*. Weighing in at around five pounds and containing 685 pages of relatively dry material, it became an unlikely bestseller, with over 2.5 million copies sold as of April 2019.[65] With its chronicling of cycles of capital accumulation (and destruction) through history and its examination of the causes of the unequal distribution of capital, it clearly struck a chord with a group of readers who are concerned about disparities in wealth.

While some of the book's conclusions about the reasons for a growing wealth gap have been debated and remain unsettled, there's no denying the overall trend. In his 2018 book *A Template for Understanding Big Debt Crises*, hedge fund manager Ray Dalio observes that the United States has nearly reached the point at which the top 0.1% of the U.S. population owns as much wealth as the bottom 90% (see Figure 4). This hasn't happened since the 1930s. The 1930s was a period of rising populism, a trend we observe today as anti-establishment candidates gain power in much of the western world.

The 1930s period encompassed the Great Depression and culminated, not coincidentally, in the deadliest war in world history. It also marked a short-term maximum level for debt in the United States, as the country experienced defaults and bankruptcies. At present, popular discontent about wealth distribution seems to be rising—apparently due to wealth concentration levels not seen since the 1930s, as illustrated in Figure 4. But this time around, the ratio of total debt to GDP in the United States is much higher than in the 1930s (see Figure 5 repeated from Chapter 3). The story is even worse in the rest of the world. The debt to GDP ratio globally is even higher now than it was on the eve of the Global Financial Crisis of 2008–2009.[66]

How might this debt disaster play out? In the next chapter, we'll consider some possibilities.

Figure 4: US Net Wealth Shares in the Last Century

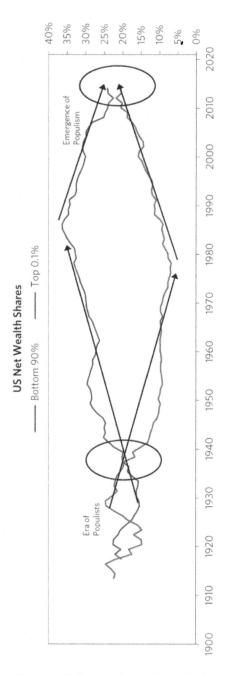

Source: A Template for Understanding Big Debt Crises by Ray Dalio, pg 31

Figure 5: US Total Debt Burdens ($GDP)

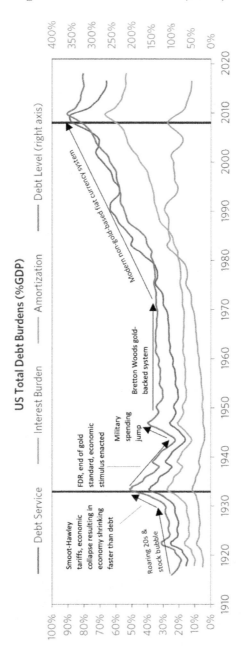

Data and Graph Source: A Template for Understanding Big Debt Crises, Ray Dalio, pg 13; Text Source: Andy Edstrom

Chapter 5

Approaching the Endgame

The Menu

There are six obvious ways to deal with excess debt: (1) austerity, (2) mass defaults, (3) jubilee (debt cancellation), (4) redistribution, (5) financial repression, and (6) consumer price inflation. We will examine these options here. They are not mutually exclusive but are usefully treated separately before we consider possible combinations.

1. Austerity, colloquially known as "belt-tightening," means cutting consumption. If you reduce consumption, you can use a greater portion of income to repay debt and reduce the debt load. Unfortunately, austerity is painful. Like dieting, it usually fails. We have seen that attempts to cut spending, especially at the government level, succumb to the demands of special interest groups and average citizens who benefit from spending. Elected politicians have to keep dishing out the goods in order to stay in office. Recent history provides a few exceptions, such as the semi-successful (so far) case of Greece, which has endured a long and deep austerity-induced recession after accumulating unsustainable debts. It remains to be seen whether Greece will be able to maintain spending reforms. It seems highly likely that if Greece weren't part of the euro area and therefore had the ability to print its own currency, it would have chosen money printing and inflation rather than austerity.

2. Mass defaults are arguably as painful as austerity because anyone who holds debt as an asset (i.e., anyone who is a lender) is made poorer when only a fraction of the debt can be repaid. The suffering is not limited to the lenders, because they are often employers who have to either lay off or reduce the pay of their workers. This situation occurred in the Great Depression of the 1930s, and voters and politicians will likely not tolerate such an event again. The Global Financial Crisis of 2008–2009 demonstrated that when the economy freezes due to problems with debt, governments will deficit-spend and print money in order to avert mass defaults in the short term.

3. Jubilee (debt cancellation) is a phenomenon that occurred in Biblical times.[67] A new ruler would ascend to power and celebrate his rise by decreeing outstanding debts null and void. Needless to say, this curried favor with the majority of the population since most people were debtors rather than lenders. The concept is appealing, but unfortunately it looks a lot like the mass defaults (and depression) scenario described in the previous paragraph. One man's debt is another man's asset, so although extinguishing debt helps the debtor, it hurts the lender.

This is disruptive to overall economic output. Furthermore, it deals a strong blow to two of the linchpins of functional economies (and societies): consistent rule of law, including contract law, and property rights. If the sovereign can declare debts null and void, it's not a large leap to decree the reallocation of property. This can be a popular policy in the short term, but it severely hampers long-term economic growth since entrepreneurs will cease to take risks if the fruits of their efforts can be capriciously stolen by the state.

4. Redistribution, or taxing the rich and giving to the rest including the indebted (whether individuals or the government), is another way to reduce aggregate debt. As I write this book, a 29-year-old member of Congress is making headlines by proposing a maximum income tax rates of 70%. While such high taxation levels are not unprecedented in U.S. history,[68] they are a historical rarity, and it's not difficult to imagine high-earners going to great lengths to avoid such punitive rates. In the 2016 presidential election, Senator Bernie Sanders made a pretty strong bid for the nomination to become the Democratic Party's presidential candidate. One of his key policies was free college for all. The popularity of candidates such as these shouldn't surprise us. If taxpayers are going to support a generation that is eligible for Social Security benefits starting at age 66 and will likely collect them for 25 years in retirement, why not pay for college for all the 20-year-olds? I would not be surprised to see higher tax rates, but the rich are powerful, and the mobility of capital and the expertise of their lawyers and money managers will allow them to come up with clever ways of avoiding tax.

5. Financial repression, a term coined by Stanford economists Edward Shaw[69] and Ronald McKinnon,[70] can include a raft of government policies designed to deliver savers an artificially low rate of interest on savings. This can be accomplished by implementing capital controls and other policies that prevent money from "leaving" the system. Such policies are currently in force in countries such as China. Bank accounts in China provide very low rates of return.[71] By making it difficult to move money out of China, the government has been able to largely keep wealth in the country, albeit at the cost of inflating a real estate bubble. Without capital controls, keeping interest rates artificially low is difficult because capital tends to be mobile and will shift overseas in search of higher investment returns.

However, central banks all over the world have so far managed to largely lower interest rates in concert (see Figure 6). These days, as illustrated in the chart, major countries' government bond yields are at or near zero. Ten-year U.S. government bonds yield about 2.4%. Ten-year British bonds yield 1.1%, and 10-year German government bonds and 10-year Japanese government bonds both yield *negative* 0.1%. Such coordinated efforts to keep interest rates low globally help mitigate the capital flight problem since there is almost nowhere to go to capture a low-risk rate of return.

Figure 6: Major Country Government 10-Year Bond Yields Since End of Bretton Woods Gold Standard

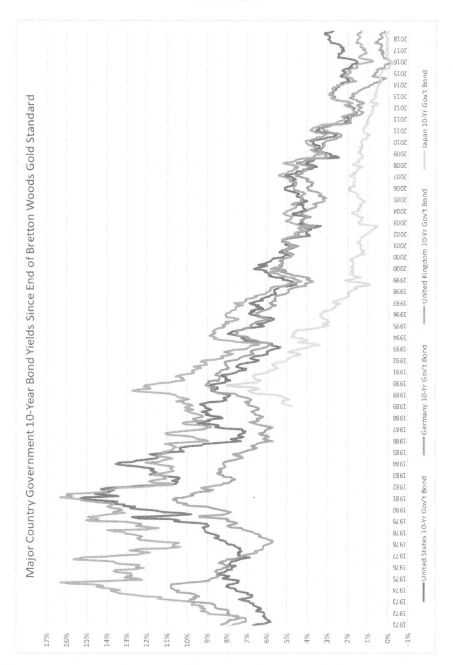

Source: Federal Reserve Economic Data,https://fred.stlouisfed.org

6. Consumer price inflation is the most likely path out of crushing debt. As discussed earlier, the standard economic model of the wage-price inflation spiral means that printing money and lowering interest rates ad infinitum should cause consumer price inflation. But globalization and automation have countered the wage-price inflation in the U.S. while inflating asset prices. And higher asset prices have made those assets more leverageable. Given that 10-year government bond yield (interest rates) have gone negative in major economies like Japan and Germany and are in the low single digits in others, what happens in the next global economic recession? It seems most likely that central banks will do what they have done in each prior cycle: lower interest rates and print money! But this time around, that will mean *negative* interest rates, including possibly on bank deposit accounts.

Skeptics I talk to argue that taking interest rates below zero will cause people to opt out and just hold cash. But with fiat currencies such as we have today, holding cash is impractical for many people because of the limitations on security and transferability over distance. Are you really going to give up your checkbook and carry wads of cash around to pay your mortgage or your rent? So in a fiat currency-based world, it is entirely possible that we will see significantly negative interest rates across the world.

Which Way Out?

Given the pros and cons described above, it seems to me that among the unappetizing options of (1) austerity, (2) mass defaults, (3) jubilee (debt cancellation), (4) redistribution, (5) financial repression, and (6) consumer price inflation, the governments and central banks of the world will order mostly from the bottom half of the menu. Voters won't tolerate (1) austerity or (2) mass defaults, and (3) a jubilee (debt cancellation) would be too damaging to contract law and property rights. Voters will likely implement more (4) redistribution, but this will be difficult as the rich can move their capital offshore in the event of confiscatory tax regimes, and they may be successful in lobbying against high taxes. (5) Financial repression, marked by negative interest rates, will likely be more palatable. If such extreme policy finally causes a significant rise in (6) consumer price inflation, so be it. Faced with a world drowning in debt, the Federal Reserve and the rest will likely tolerate 5%–8% consumer price inflation to reduce the "real" burden of debts if that's what's required to avoid austerity and mass defaults.

The Federal Reserve is already laying the groundwork for lower interest rates today. On May 1, 2019, the Federal Open Market Committee (FOMC) issued its periodic statement.[72] More prominent than usual was its use of the word "symmetric" with respect to its 2% annual inflation goal. This highlights the fact that the Fed's mandate is to hit 2% inflation on average, which means that for every year it falls short of 2%, it should *overshoot* 2% in another year to make up the difference over time. Given that the Federal Reserve has undershot its inflation targets for years now (at least by its systematically understated measurement methods described earlier), it is highlighting the idea that it could reasonably seek to overshoot its 2% target for years to make up for lost ground. This implies keeping interest rates lower for longer.

The political domain is also moving toward lower interest rates. At the time of this writing, there is ongoing discussion among some members of Congress about the virtues of Modern Monetary Theory,[73] which holds that governments can run budget deficits forever since they can print money forever to fund them. This is true, unless you want your currency to actually maintain its purchasing power. In a world without usable alternatives to the fiat currency-based banking system, savers might be stuck with governments forever debasing their money. But thanks to Bitcoin, for the first time in history there is a usable alternative. We will begin to examine this alternative in Chapter 7.

First, however, we must delve another layer deeper into the question of "What Is Money?" Specifically, what makes something a *good* form of money? Analyzing the characteristics of good money will allow us to compare and contrast fiat money (in the form of the dollar), gold, and, ultimately, Bitcoin.

Chapter 6

What Is Money *Really*?

In Chapter 2 we examined Carl Menger's framework for defining money and its use primarily as a medium of exchange. Chapters 3–5 described the monetary and debt system as it exists today. I hope it left you with some significant doubts about the state of our existing financial system. Now it's time to peel the monetary onion further to glimpse money's fundamental core, which will help illuminate why some of the root problems with this system relate to characteristics of the fiat currency system that has been adopted throughout the world.

The 14 Characteristics of Good Money

As we established, money is fundamentally a medium of exchange. But what makes something a *good* medium of exchange? What causes it to accrue a monetary premium? It appears that moneyness is an *emergent* phenomenon that depends on the aggregation and interaction of a collection of lower-level properties. Aristotle is credited with proposing that money is durable, divisible, portable, and intrinsically valuable.[74] This definition is a good start but still omits the majority of the factors that I believe define money. To my mind, good money has no fewer than 14 important characteristics. Furthermore, *no form of money in the history of civilization scores highly on all of these factors—not a single one.* This means that each form of money that has been used in society has strengths and weaknesses among its various characteristics. Here are my 14 Characteristics of Good Money.

1. Identifiable. Any time you are selling a good or service for money, you need to be able to identify the money you are receiving. The most usable money will be easily identifiable, because this reduces the work required for the seller to verify that she is receiving the amount of value for her merchandise that she thinks she is. Accepting money that isn't valid results in the merchandise seller being defrauded. Such an outcome can occur due to negligence (the seller accidentally accepting a ten-dollar bill in place of a twenty-dollar bill) or due to a buyer attempting to purchase the merchandise using counterfeit money (whether a home-printed bill or a lump of fool's gold). No form of money that is difficult to identify or easy to fake will succeed.

2. Transferable. Since money is first and foremost a medium of exchange, you must be able to efficiently transfer it to someone else and thereby transmit value.

3. Durable. Durability is important for transacting across both space and time. Money that is delicate and cannot survive travel is not very useful. Neither is money that is perishable. A staple crop that can rot or a metal that easily rusts or tarnishes is of limited use as money.

4. Divisible. In order to achieve salability across scale (see Chapter 2), money must be divisible into small units of value so that it can be exchanged for low-value goods and services and so that higher-value goods and services can be priced precisely. A type of rare shell used as money that is worth twice as much as a single book cannot be used to purchase the book. Likewise, a hundred-dollar bill is a very inconvenient way to buy a gallon of milk.

5. Dense. For money to be useful for sizable purchases, it must be relatively dense in value. A substance such as sand is quite divisible into individual grains that each have very small amounts of value, but those units are so low-value that even a great number of them in aggregate isn't valuable enough to use as money.

6. Scarce. Throughout history, one of the major killers of currencies has been excess supply. The result is price inflation. A money whose value can easily be diluted due to increase in supply is doomed. Any successful money must be difficult to create. Its creation must therefore be costly. "Unforgeable costliness", a key concept we will address later in this chapter is therefore crucial to any money's long-term success.

7. Short-Term Stable Value. Even if it doesn't lose purchasing power over the long term, a money whose purchasing power jumps up and down in the short term is of limited use. A money's purchasing power is effectively its price, which is set by the balance of supply and demand for the money. Short-term supply/demand imbalances that dramatically move the money's price (and therefore the prices of all goods and services in terms of the money) make the money less effective as a medium of exchange.

8. Long-Term Stable Value. Short-term price stability is useful for transactions across space and scale, but not across significant periods of time. Storing value in money in order to purchase a good or service at a much later date requires long-term price stability.

9. Fungible. Fungibility means that one piece of money of a given stated value is the same as all the others of that stated value. All units should be identical such that one piece can substitute for another, and no particular piece is deemed better or tainted. Precious stones like diamonds would be superior forms of money if each stone were not unique. The fact that there are differences between each individual stone requires the seller of the good or service to assess the value of the gem being offered, which significantly reduces ease of exchange.

10. Unseizable. Transferability is a double-edged sword. Money that can be transferred away from you without your consent (i.e., seized) is not as good as money that is hard to seize. The best money is resistant to parties who seek to seize it, including thieves, sticky-fingered border guards, invading armies, and corrupt tax collectors.

11. Censorship-Resistant. The type of transferability envisioned in the earlier definition is based on mutual consent by both the seller and the buyer of the good or service. As surely as a third party taking your money from you without your consent is a problem, so is a third party preventing you from engaging in a transaction to which both buyer and seller of a good or service have consented. You probably don't want a third party to have the power to stop you from transferring the money to someone.

12. Private. Most of us don't want every action we take (whether intimate, exciting, or mundane) to be broadcast to the world. Just as we would like to occasionally communicate privately, we sometimes need to transact privately. You might not mind having some of your purchases broadcast to the world, but you probably want to at least have the option of privacy on occasion.

13. Required for Some Important Purpose. One effective way of bolstering a form of money is to make sure it's required for some purpose. Governments who require their native currency for payment of taxes are a good example. But a business can also create demand for its particular money by requiring its use when purchasing its goods or services, such as a laundromat that requires you to buy customer tokens to operate the washing machines, or a carnival that requires the purchase of tickets to spend on rides.

14. Backed by a Powerful Agent. It helps if a powerful agent or group of agents (such as a government) explicitly or implicitly supports it. Probably the greatest strength of the U.S. dollar is that it is backed by the world's most powerful military. However, backing by a powerful agent can also be double-edged if it means less censorship-resistance and greater seizability.

Since no existing form of money scores highly on all of the above factors, it's understandable that there are multiple forms of money in existence with different "scores" in the different categories. Let's examine one modern form of money and one more ancient form of money and see how they rank. I score each category on a 0–5 scale, with 5 being the highest.

U.S. Dollar

Identifiable. 4 out of 5. Most people know more or less what cash bills look like. However, a portion of the bills in circulation are counterfeit. Electronic dollars can also be fraudulent in certain cases (as with debit card and credit card fraud).

Transferable. 4 out of 5. Physical cash is highly transferable, except you have to hand it off in person. "Cash" in a bank account (which is really a demand deposit) is highly transferable, except you have to pay a fee for large transfers, and such transfers take at least 24 hours to settle domestically and several days to settle internationally.

Durable. 4 out of 5. Physical cash bills are somewhat sturdy, and coins more so, but coins don't store much value since they are low-denomination almost everywhere. Bank deposits are subject to the functioning of banks' centralized information technology systems and also inter-bank payments/settlement systems including SWIFT (the Society for the Worldwide Interbank Financial Telecommunication).

Divisible. 4 out of 5. There aren't many things that require payment of less than a penny. However, when paying for something using electronic dollars (via the banking or credit card systems) dollar payments effectively aren't divisible to much less than a few dollars apiece because of minimum charges imposed by the payment systems. This appears to be the key reason that "micropayments" don't exist in the United States today.

Dense. 4 out of 5. While the U.S. dollar allows for units as small as a penny, it also allows for relatively high value density through the hundred-dollar bill. A million dollars' worth of hundreds can easily fit into a briefcase or backpack.

Scarce. 2 out of 5. The Federal Reserve tries to partially limit the supply of dollars, but it printed *over $4 trillion* worth after the Global Financial Crisis of 2008–2009. Every single fiat currency in history has ultimately been debased to a fraction of its original value. Currencies that are scarce tend to be more resilient in the long run.

Fungible. 4 out of 5. Generally speaking, a dollar is a dollar is a dollar. However, there are certain cases in which dollars are "tainted" (e.g., when stolen from a bank and hurriedly spent). Also, some people won't accept badly damaged or overworn bills.

Short-Term Stable Value. 5 out of 5. In the short term (e.g., today versus last month) the dollar's value is quite stable. If you're not ready to spend your dollars until next month, you don't lose too much by holding them.

Long-Term Stable Value. 3 out of 5. In the long term, the dollar consistently loses purchasing power. Inflation has debased the dollar dramatically over the decades. Its value has held up better than those of many other fiat currencies, but that's a pretty low bar to clear.

Unseizable. 2 out of 5. Bank deposits can be frozen or expropriated by the government. Cash can be seized if not extraordinarily well-hidden.

Censorship-Resistant. 3 out of 5. Physical cash bills are relatively censorship-resistant, provided the user isn't under surveillance. But it's hard to move lots of cash if you're being watched. Payments through the banking system are certainly not censorship-resistant, as the government can prevent, freeze, or even reverse payments.

Private. 3 out of 5. Physical bills are generally an effective way of transacting privately, unless you are under surveillance at the time of the transaction. Another way privacy (and fungibility) can be foiled is by marking bills. Payments through the banking system are not private, since the government can easily monitor such payments.

Required for Some Important Purpose. 5 out of 5. The U.S. government requires citizens to use dollars to settle tax liabilities.

Backed by a Powerful Agent. 5 out of 5. The dollar is backed by the full faith and credit of the U.S. government, which is backed by the strongest military in the world.

U.S. Dollar Total Score: 52 points out of a possible 70. Pretty good.

Gold

Identifiable. 3 out of 5. A lot of people know more or less what gold looks like and how hard it is (hence the old trick of biting it to test its hardness). However, many people would not be willing to accept a payment in gold without an expert on hand to verify its authenticity.

Transferable. 3 out of 5. Gold is compact and can be carried, though the amount of value that can be conveyed this way is limited. It cannot be sent electronically, and it cannot be sent securely over long distances without great expense for shipping and security.

Durable. 5 out of 5. Gold is inert and can survive physical and chemical abuse far better than most materials.

Divisible. 2 out of 5. It's not easy to carve up a block of gold, and it's especially tough to divide it into pieces of value small enough that they are useful for everyday purchases. Even gold coins aren't usually small-enough in denomination to be useful for buying a sandwich.

Dense. 4 out of 5. A 400-ounce gold bar is worth over half a million dollars assuming $1,300 per ounce of gold. At 25 pounds apiece, two bars can store a million dollars in 50 pounds of weight in a space that is smaller than a suitcase full of hundred-dollar bills but also heavier.

Scarce. 4 out of 5. There is ongoing gold mining, but that adds less than 2% to world supply annually.

Fungible. 3 out of 5. Chemically, pure gold is fully fungible. Unfortunately, it's difficult to tell on the spot how pure it is, which makes it difficult to substitute gold in different physical forms.

Short-Term Stable Value. 3 out of 5. Gold's price is somewhat volatile in the short term and frequently sees weekly movements in its purchasing power of several percentage points.

Long-Term Stable Value. 5 out of 5. Gold seems to have kept its purchasing power over centuries and even millennia. One popular metric is that an ounce of gold (today around $1,300) has purchased a man's suit over the ages, whether at Brooks Brothers in New York today or at a toga retailer in Rome two thousand years ago.[75]

Unseizable. 2 out of 5. Gold can be hidden, but protecting it reliably from seizure requires taking significant security measures. Good luck getting it past the border guard if you have to flee the country.

Censorship-Resistant. 3 out of 5. If someone wants to transact in gold, it's hard to stop them, but they have to do it physically and in person.

Private. 3 out of 5. As with dollars, gold transactions via intermediaries, such as a gold fund or a gold vault provider, are not private, since the government can easily monitor such payments. Like dollar bills, gold coins can be traded privately unless they are surveilled, tracked, or marked. However, unmarked gold bullion traded physically is harder to track.

Required for Some Important Purpose. 3 out of 5. People the world over demand it, though such demand varies by country and often other substances (diamonds, silver) can substitute. Governments hold significant reserves, but only a fraction of the value of the total supply.

Backed by a Powerful Agent. 3 out of 5. Central banks buy/own/support gold in significant amounts, albeit less than when there was an official monetary gold standard.

Gold Total Score: 46 points out of a possible 70. Not as good as dollars, but better in certain categories and overall not bad.

The foregoing analysis is undoubtedly flawed and simplistic, not least because of the following limitations:

(A) The 0–5 scale has only six possible levels and therefore lacks precision.

(B) Reasonable people can disagree on the right score for each factor.

(C) Each factor is given equal weight, but some factors are likely more important than others, although this may depend on the user's preferences (more on that later).

Nevertheless, this analysis highlights the important characteristics of good money, and it illustrates that some forms of money score better on certain characteristics than others. Moreover, since different people have different preferences, different forms of money can appeal to different people.

Just over a decade ago, a new form of money that is based on open-source software and native to the Internet was introduced to the world. In the next chapter we will see how it compares to the dollar and gold with respect to the 14 Characteristics of Good Money. But first we will augment our monetary toolset with a few more useful frameworks for analysis.

Money as Ledger

In Chapter 2 we noted that money must act as a medium of exchange, and to achieve this it must be a "store of value." To accomplish this task, it must effectively act as a ledger. It's easy to conceive of electronic bank account balances as a giant ledger that tracks who owns which amount of money. But physical U.S. dollar bills are also a sort of ledger since physical possession of the notes tracks ownership of a portion of the global total. Physical gold functions as a ledger also, as people know that extracting gold is expensive and that increases in its supply are limited to less than 2% annually (more on this later). A person who wears gold jewelry is effectively signaling to the public her ownership of a portion of her "account" on the global "gold ledger." Monetary systems have always been ledgers that keep track of purchasing power, whether in (1) a computer database (as with a bank account today), or (2) a handwritten database (as with bank and merchant accounts hundreds of years ago), or (3) physical possession of gold coins or jewelry thousands of years ago.

Money as Story and Social Consensus

Perhaps nobody in recent history has done more than Yuval Harari to illuminate the governing dynamics of the human species. One of his key ideas is that the characteristic of humankind that has allowed our species to dominate the world is the ability to believe in stories that drive a social consensus. This is the only factor that allows "teamwork" among a group of people larger than about 150 (the "Dunbar number" cited in Chapter 1). If you are only able to cooperate with someone you know on a personal level, you won't be able to cooperate with very many people, and you will never be able to construct a pyramid or engineer a modern airplane or deliver a package anywhere in the country within 24 hours. But if you can believe in a story that creates a social consensus and if others do the same, then you can create a large team to achieve a complex endeavor.

The concept of stories extends to many of the major social abstractions that literally govern our daily lives. For example, try handing someone a piece of the U.S. government. I am writing this book in my home office, which has at least a five-mile view of the city to the west since I live on a hill. Even from this perch, I can't see any U.S. government anywhere around me. But the social consensus around the story of the U.S. government's existence and legitimacy lives in the minds of over 300 million Americans, and this social consensus powers the world's biggest economy.

One way to think about the story and associated social consensus is that the story includes the origin, which is then expressed in the detailed consensus. The story is often simple and principles-based. It exists in people's minds. But the detailed consensus is often more complex, and in order for it to function, it must be explicitly codified and recorded. To flesh out the details, it must be written down. The story of the United States that we have agreed to believe in is that it originated in the attempt to escape oppression by a distant hegemon and was loosely defined by concepts such as liberty. That fuzzy idea was then codified in the Articles of Confederation, and later amended into the Constitution, which was itself subsequently amended numerous times.

Money, too, is a story about which we have woven a social consensus. The most popular forms of money have little or no value other than as money. This is true for the dollar, which has almost no non-monetary value. It is also true for gold, which for centuries had almost no non-monetary value other than decoration, and later developed modest industrial uses, which still pale in comparison to gold's monetary value. Once a form of money achieves status as money and accrues a monetary premium, it tends to maintain that monetary premium for a significant period of time as the social consensus around it attains a certain durability. A key source of the durability of this consensus is money's characteristic of being a protocol.

Money as Protocol

It has been argued that money is speech. Leaving aside legal definitions of speech, money certainly exhibits characteristics of language. While spoken or written language is a system for transmitting information, money is a language for transmitting *value*. Language has a "network effect"; the more people that use the same language, the more useful (and therefore valuable) that language is. This increase in value is true not just in aggregate, but also *per user*.

Nations and peoples have their own languages. However, the most successful people learn not only their native language, but also that of the global hegemon at the time. Whether Latin, Spanish, French, or English, there has for large portions of history been a common language used across nations. Partly this is a result of imposition by the dominant military and cultural power of the age. But aside from the threat of violence, a key driver of common language usage is the huge economic efficiencies realized by sharing a language. Notwithstanding the rise and fall of various superpowers over centuries, national languages have also succeeded within their borders due to the efficiency benefits of coordination. Any emperor could tell you that governing lands populated by people who do not speak the same language is difficult, and this fact has been known at least since the Biblical story of the Tower of Babel.

As with governing or coordinating people who speak disparate languages, conducting commerce is inefficient if you are saddled with many different currencies. Paying the butcher with a different currency than you pay the baker is cumbersome. Taken to an extreme, we can imagine a world in which each person has her own personal currency. In exchange for a copy of my book, I demand Andybucks, and in order to buy goods at Target I have to swap my Andybucks for Targetbucks. Then Target trades away its Target-bucks to pay its employees each in their own personal currencies. This world looks similar to the Tower of Babel story, in which everyone speaks a different language and therefore cannot communicate with each other.

As we observe many of the same "network effects" arising from using the same money as from using the same language, what becomes evident is that both money and language are characterized by networks. But both money and language are also protocols. Merriam-Webster's online dictionary includes several definitions of a protocol. Generally, a protocol is a *set of procedures or rules for acting*. In the context of participants in a network, that means a set of procedures or rules for network participants *interacting with each other*. Thinking about money as a type of protocol for interacting within a network is useful because it highlights the issue of network effects and other characteristics that we will explore later.

Today the U.S. dollar is a protocol on which numerous higher-level systems are built. These higher-level structures include the payments system; the banking system, which in turn includes the subsystems of mortgage lending, consumer lending (through credit cards and other instruments), and a portion of the market for corporate lending; the petrodollar system, whereby most oil contracts are priced in dollars; the world's largest corporate bond market; and the world's largest government bond market. All of these systems are denominated in dollars and depend on the dollar as a base protocol.

For something to become used widely as a monetary protocol, a social consensus must first develop among its users. Such a social consensus does not arrive out of thin air. It arises from the set of fundamental characteristics identified earlier as the 14 Characteristics of Good Money.

Scarcity from Unforgeable Costliness

Digital currency pioneer Nick Szabo defines scarcity as "unforgeable costliness."[76] According to Szabo, this can be achieved by an object via either the "improbability of [its] history" or its "original cost." Improbability of history explains why asteroids are scarce. Space rocks don't hit the earth's surface very often. Historical artifacts, antiques, and other collectibles are scarce because there are a limited number of objects relevant to major historical events. But for most objects, scarcity arises from the fact that it is expensive to create or acquire the object. Practically, this expense of creation or acquisition arises from the energy required for creation or acquisition. The Great Pyramid of Giza in Egypt is obviously a scarce item because it's clear that cutting, moving, and stacking 50-ton stone blocks is a very costly and energy-intensive exercise. There is little doubt that a significant economy was harnessed to create the Great Pyramid. Its very existence is proof of expenditure of vast amounts of energy (i.e., a "proof of work") and evidence of unforgeable costliness and therefore scarcity.

If you're married, chances are good that you have experience with unforgeable costliness and scarcity. The diamond ring that cost thousands of dollars isn't merely a beautiful trinket. It could easily have been replaced by a plastic one that fools the untrained eye, or even a lab-manufactured one that fools the chemist's well-trained eye, since lab-grown gems are chemically identical to the gems found in the ground. But such substitutes for a diamond pulled out of the earth are not scarce because they are not unforgeably costly to produce. For many brides, only a scarce and unforgeably costly *mined* diamond will do.

Diamonds are somewhat of a money substitute, and in a world without better options, they might feature more prominently as money. However, they are significantly hampered by their lack of fungibility (since each diamond is unique), limited divisibility (since it's tough to make small change in diamonds), and difficult identifiability (since it's possible to pass fake ones off as real to the untrained eye). But there are other scarce and unforgeably costly physical things that come out of the earth that have been among the most popular forms of money for millennia: monetary metals.

Monetary Metals

Monetary metals score well on the 14 Characteristics of Good Money. As a result, they have enjoyed a long and complex history as money. This history extends far beyond the scope of this book, and other writers have catalogued it exhaustively. But we will hit a few key points because they underscore the 14 Characteristics of Good Money.

There have been periods in history in which multiple metals served as money, including gold, silver, and copper. Gold won in the long run for a few key reasons. Relative to other monetary metals such as silver and copper, the primary reason for gold's long-term success seems to have been its very high *stock-to-flow ratio.*[77] Most metals have stock-to-flow ratios of around one or less. That means that in a given year, the amount of stockpiled inventory of the metal is approximately equal to the amount that was produced over the course of the year. This implies that people consume the metal almost as quickly as it can be produced. Gold stands in stark contrast to "industrial" metals that have low stock-to-flow ratios. Because of its few industrial uses (it doesn't get "used up") and the fact that gold has been mined for thousands of years, above-ground stockpiles of gold are enormous compared to annual new production. Such annual production has not accounted for more than 2% of the existing above-ground stock since 1942.[78] This means that gold's stock-to-flow ratio exceeds one divided by 2%, which is to say that it exceeds 50.

This huge stock-to-flow ratio means that incremental supply is extremely *inelastic* to price. If an increase in demand for the metal causes the price to rise in the short term, suppliers cannot flood the market with supply and crash the price. For example, if the price of gold doubles tomorrow and new supply also doubles, as excited gold producers open new mines or re-open previously idled ones, the annual production will still be less than 4% of the existing stock. In contrast, a doubling in the price of copper could cause an overreaction on the supply side, resulting in annual production as a percent of the existing stock jumping from 100% to 200%. Such a huge increase in supply could tank the price. Indeed, history demonstrates that industrial metals such as copper experience large fluctuations in supply and in price. Gold's relative immunity to such outcomes has cemented its place as the monetary metal of choice.

Embedded in this dynamic is the underappreciated fact emphasized in Chapter 2 that the best money is something that is useless as anything other than money. Therefore, a commodity that has significant industrial utility actually makes a *worse* money than a thing that has little or no industrial utility. This is because any commodity with industrial uses generally gets consumed almost as quickly as it is produced, which prevents the accumulation of a significant stock of the commodity over time. This results in very low stock-to-flow ratios that can result in huge fluctuations in supply that cause huge fluctuations in price. Such large fluctuations in price make industrial metals bad stores of value and therefore ineffective media of exchange across time. Based on Bloomberg data, gold's average monthly price volatility over the last 40 years measured by standard deviation of price change is 5.3%. For silver and copper, the figures are 10.1% and 10.7%, respectively. Therefore, silver and copper each have price volatility measured by monthly standard deviation in price movements that are roughly double that of gold.

Another reason for gold's greater success as money than silver or copper is its durability. Gold is almost completely inert and, therefore, does not corrode over time. In contrast, silver and copper tarnish or rust over time. Additionally, gold has been favored over silver or copper because of its higher value density due to its greater scarcity. Fewer ounces of gold have been discovered in Earth's crust than of silver or copper. This has helped achieve a value per ounce that is much higher than those of silver or copper.

This high value density is a double-edged sword. One of the key reasons that silver and copper have been used as money historically is that they can be coined into smaller amounts of value. They score better than gold on Characteristic of Good Money #4: Divisible. This makes them better media of exchange *across scale* than gold. Silver especially proved resilient as a monetary metal on and off for centuries, but its death knell came with the spread of gold-backed paper currency. Such gold-backed paper money took advantage of gold's immense stock-to-flow ratio and resultant short-term and long-term price stability, while also allowing the printing of small denomination notes that facilitated transacting at low levels of value.

Fiat Money as a Regressive Taxation System

In the last few centuries, gold-backed paper money systems were not uncommon, with the most recent manifestation being the 27 years of the Bretton Woods system (1944-1971). Unfortunately for their citizens, governments realized that they could centralize the custody of gold in vaults, and once they had done so, it was too tempting to move to a fractional reserve system. A government that could print $20 bills at a cost of 10 cents each could collect the difference as profit, known as "seigniorage." This potential profit was too enticing to resist.

For a time, these systems allowed governments to take advantage of the seigniorage they generated by running fractional reserve gold-backed paper money systems. Users were technically allowed to redeem their paper notes for gold, but the central bank didn't have enough gold to satisfy all claims. Ultimately, these fractional reserve gold-backed paper money systems failed as noteholders sought to redeem their notes for gold, knowing that if they didn't, someone else might redeem their stake and leave the rest of claimants without any golden collateral to claim. Governments can't seem to resist the temptation of printing free money (notes/claims) "backed" by gold until the gold backing is so diluted that noteholders demand their gold back and the edifice crumbles in a classic "bank run." When Richard Nixon announced the "temporary" (ultimately permanent) end of the Bretton Woods gold-backed paper money system on August 15, 1971, it was effectively the end of gold-backed money in the modern era. From that moment onward, governments have been able to print money at near-zero expense and without the potential discipline imposed by the threat of holders demanding gold in exchange for their paper claims.

Today, this seigniorage, which is really a stealth tax, amounts to roughly $20 billion annually for the U.S. dollar.[79] Unfortunately, this stealth tax is *regressive*. The rich, who have accumulated assets, have greater access to higher-return investments (the capital goods described in Chapter 2) than the poor do. This occurs for the simple reason that everyone must maintain at least some amount of money just to function in society, since operating in a modern economy requires transacting. This "working capital" required to buy groceries and pay the rent must be held as money, which under a fiat system loses its purchasing power via the stealth tax of seigniorage. Those people who have been able to accumulate some surplus wealth can invest it in capital goods with positive expected returns. But the poor who can accumulate only enough capital to fund their working capital needs (by holding money) see the value of that capital fall every year.

It is therefore the poor who suffer more from the stealth seigniorage tax than the rich. Certain candidates for political office have recently been calling for a wealth tax as a progressive tool for redistributing assets from the rich to the poor.[80] Unfortunately, we already have an inflationary seigniorage wealth tax on money *that does the opposite by hitting the poor hardest.*

Fiat Money as Regressive Subsidy to the Banking Industry, Corporations, and the Rich

While monetary inflation is a regressive tax that hits the poor hardest as a percentage of their income and wealth, proponents of this system label it "fair" based on the logic that all dollars are effectively taxed by seigniorage at the same percentage. Seventeenth-century economist Richard Cantillon recognized the folly of this argument,[81] and Mises later articulated it further in *Human Action*.[82] While it's true that over time printing money will result in a general rise in the price level of goods and services in the economy, *it doesn't happen simultaneously across goods and services.*

For example, when the central bank creates new money, it flows first to the financial system and primarily the banks. They are given the privilege of being the first to take those dollars into their reserves and then lend them to the businesses they think will offer the greatest risk-adjusted return to the bank. In turn, the businesses owners (capitalists) who receive those loans can make more capital expenditures and pay their workers more. This results in those workers being able to pay more for goods and services and bid up the prices thereon. So, the bankers get the money first, then the business owners, and last the workers. Considering that bankers and business owners tend to be wealthier than wage-earning workers, the system creates *another* regressive effect.

Another major subsidy that flows from the Federal Reserve to the broader banking system is the payment of interest on bank reserves held at the Federal

Reserve. Currently, the Federal Reserve pays banks 2.35% annualized interest on funds that a bank deposits at the Federal Reserve. Such deposits are free of default risk since the Federal Reserve can always print money to satisfy such obligations. As of May 2019 the amount of reserves that depository institutions (mainly banks) were required to hold at the Federal Reserve was $200 billion. But the amount that institutions deposited in excess of that minimum was $1.368 *trillion*.[83] Last I checked, the checking and savings accounts that I maintain at major national banks are paying me less than 0.1% interest or less. Effectively, the banks can hold my deposits, pay me 0.1% interest, and lend my money to the Federal Reserve risk-free to earn a 2.25% net interest margin. Applying this 2.25% net interest margin to the $1.568 trillion of total reserves ($200 billion minimum reserves plus $1.368 trillion excess reserves) implies a subsidy to the banking system of over $35 billion annually!

It's interesting that a group of businesspeople recently attempted to open what's known as a "narrow bank." Under this business plan, the bank would limit itself to one function only: taking its customers' deposits and depositing them with the Federal Reserve to earn the 2.35% the Federal Reserve is paying. No business loans, no mortgages, or other typical bank activities—just collect the 2.35% from the Fed, take a cut for expenses and profits, and pass the rest to depositors. An actual company called the Narrow Bank filed its application in August 2017.[84] Almost two years later, the Federal Reserve has not approved the application.[85] I suspect it's because it shines a spotlight on the Fed's blatant giveaway to the banking system.

The Fed's outright subsidy to the banking system is just one of the signals of the dysfunction of the existing monetary system. The Federal Reserve subsidizes the banking system, but not the ordinary depositors, like you and me, who hold bank accounts. And if anyone tries to challenge that system and return some of the profits to the people, as the Narrow Bank group has done, the Federal Reserve succumbs to pressure from the banking industry and stalls, offering up a variety of explanations for why it is doing so that ultimately amount to "because although it would be good for you and me, it's bad for the banks."

The Federal Reserve uses inflationary seigniorage to regressively tax the poor more than the rich. It further subsidizes the rich by keeping interest rates artificially low, which raises the prices of investment assets (capital goods) that are owned primarily by the wealthy. It prices young homebuyers out of the housing market because they can't scrape together ever-rising down payments on ever-rising home prices. And it threatens to lower interest rates ever further in a misguided effort to "stimulate" the economy, which only stimulates ever-increasing debt incurrence. A decade ago, endless money printing and financial repression would have appeared inexorable. But now we have a potential solution.

It's called Bitcoin.

Chapter 7

Bitcoin Basics

Bitcoin's Birth

Last Halloween my kids (aged six and three) enjoyed their annual chance to dress up and accumulate sugary treats that for the other 364 days of the year are treated as controlled substances in my household. (At least that's how I treat them; my wife is more fun than I am.) I shared in the Halloween revelry, but I was quietly celebrating something else: Bitcoin's 10th birthday.

On October 31, 2008, a pseudonymous author named "Satoshi Nakamoto" published the whitepaper that introduced Bitcoin to the world. A couple months earlier the largest bankruptcy in history (Lehman Brothers) had been filed. Global financial markets were in freefall as investors wondered whether the entire financial system was ending. It was the first global financial crisis since the 1930s, and investors were utterly panicked.

In this crucible the world's first successful decentralized cryptocurrency was forged. On January 3, 2009, two months after the Halloween whitepaper release, the Bitcoin network went live. The first "block" of transactions that was validated by the system (the so-called genesis block that was also the first "link" in the world's first "blockchain" ledger) contained the following text:

The Times 03/Jan/2009 Chancellor on brink of second bailout for banks

"The Times" refers to the famous newspaper *The Times* of London. "Chancellor on the brink of second bailout for banks" is the front-page headline of that newspaper on that date. "Chancellor" refers to the Chancellor of the Exchequer, the British equivalent of the Treasury Secretary in the United States. The "second bailout for banks" refers to the fact that the British government had already saved some British banks from collapse and was now contemplating another round of bailouts. The day the Bitcoin network went live, the Global Financial Crisis of 2008–2009 was in full swing, and governments were struggling to save a monetary and credit system on the verge of total collapse.

As we explored in Chapters 3–5, the prevailing monetary and debt system hasn't improved much in the decade since Bitcoin's launch during the Global Financial Crisis of 2008–2009. Our understanding of what went wrong in that crisis provides us with the historical context against which to measure many of the positive attributes of Bitcoin. But history is just one of the frameworks we will apply to understand why Bitcoin may possibly be the best money the world has ever known.

Let's start by asking: what *is* Bitcoin?

Bitcoin as "The Internet of Money"

On August 20, 2011, former Internet entrepreneur and current venture capitalist Marc Andreessen wrote an op-ed in *The Wall Street Journal* entitled "Why Software is Eating the World."[86] The trend of developing software to automate processes that had previously been performed by either physical analog systems or humans, was well underway when his op-ed appeared. It hasn't slowed since.

The reasons for software's success are manifold. It has near-zero marginal cost of production. That means once it is created, it can be copied at almost no cost. Because any logical operation can be expressed in code, the "design space" for software protocols and applications is nearly infinite. Moreover, once a clever software developer comes up with a new idea in this design space, it is relatively quick and cheap to iterate and hone that new idea. In the business of making physical things, prototyping is slow and expensive. In software, it's merely a matter of thinking carefully and then typing into a keyboard. This is not to minimize the accomplishments of software designers. The best software designers create huge amounts of value. But they also undoubtedly benefit from structural features that make software an extraordinarily powerful tool. Software has become even more powerful thanks to the Internet, which brought global interconnection to the planet's computational resources, and thereby dramatically broadened software's reach across the world. It has also benefited by seemingly inexorable improvements in the computational hardware on which it runs.

Both software and the Internet are key to what makes Bitcoin such a powerful form of money. Early Bitcoin adopter and educator Andreas Antonopoulos has called Bitcoin "The Internet of Money."[87] I believe this is true in the same way that Amazon is the "Internet of Retail," and Facebook and Twitter are the "Internet of Media." This is to say that Amazon is the *Internet-native solution* for retail; Facebook and Twitter are the *Internet-native solutions* for media; and Bitcoin is the *Internet-native solution* for money. Internet-enabled software has allowed Internet-native companies to provide networked-software-based solutions for retail and for media. And now, with Bitcoin, we have the first successful case of the Internet providing a networked, software-based solution for *money.*

It's almost surprising that it has taken this long to arrive at this form of money, which Twitter and Square founder Jack Dorsey has said is destined to overtake the dollar in importance and to become the single global currency of the Internet and possibly the world.[88] Want to send a message to someone on the other side of the globe? Shoot them an email and it's there in seconds. Want to talk face-to-face with a friend across the country using live-streaming video and audio? No problem. Fire up Facetime or Skype, and you're talking almost instantly. Want to tip somebody on a website 50 cents for an article they wrote? Sorry, systems for micropayments don't exist in the United States today. Want to send $5,000 to a merchant in Europe today? Sorry, international wires take days to settle. The fastest way to deliver the money is to put it in a suitcase, drive to the airport, and fly it to the recipient.

There's no logical reason for this inability to send payments quickly over distance. Electronic money is just bits of data traveling through communications infrastructure. It's no different from any other information transmitted internationally. The Internet never had a native protocol for money—until Bitcoin. The Bitcoin network allows secure transactions of both small and large amounts anywhere in the world in less than an hour. Second-layer systems like the Lightning Network (which we'll discuss later) are likely to reduce the payment time to seconds or less.

Having defined Bitcoin as the Internet of Money, let's learn something about how it works.

Building Blocks of an Internet-Native Currency

Understanding the technological, cryptographic, economic, political, legal, psychological, and game theoretic characteristics of the Bitcoin system is not a trivial undertaking. Therefore, the following explanation of how Bitcoin works is simplified for ease of consumption.[89] It's designed to provide just enough description to allow a basic understanding of the governing dynamics of the system, and an appreciation for why it's so effective. This section necessarily includes an explanation of a few crucial computing tools. For many readers, this will be the most difficult part of the book. Don't be surprised if you have to read it a few times for it to sink in. It took me hours of research and reflection to absorb the basics, and hundreds of hours to test the logic of the system to gain comfort in its resilience. Almost nobody instantly "gets it," and the few that do tend to be professional computer scientists with specific expertise in distributed systems and cryptography.

We'll start simple. As we discussed in Chapter 6, every system of money is effectively a ledger that keeps track of who owns how much money. Bitcoin is no different. The problem with ledgers is that someone has to be trusted to maintain the ledger accurately. In the case of gold, the ledger is reflected in who has physical possession of how much gold. But if you introduce a gold-backed system with paper claims against gold, then you have to trust the custodian of the gold not to issue multiple paper claims against the same amount of gold. In the past, such trust has proven to be misplaced, and gold-based systems have failed as governments printed too many paper claims against a limited quantity of gold. There's a similar problem with fiat currencies, such as the dollar, because the government can print money at will, without regard to any limitation on supply other than the threat of runaway inflation. Chapter 3 showed us that governments don't have a very good track record of controlling their monetary printing presses.

Cryptographers and entrepreneurs struggled for decades through the 1980s, 1990s, and 2000s to devise an electronic money system that could solve the problem of the trusted third party. The reason it's so difficult to solve this problem for a digital, Internet-native currency, has to do precisely with what makes the Internet so powerful: its ability to offer data in the form of free, copiable information to everyone. Since digital currencies are based on data, and since data on the Internet can be copied at almost no cost, it is very difficult to achieve the scarcity necessary for a functional currency.

If you hand a gold coin to me as payment, that value transfer is unambiguous. You had the gold, and now you don't. I didn't have the gold, and now I do. Physical dollars work the same way. If I hand you a twenty-dollar bill, I have lost the value, and you have gained it. But digital money presents a problem. I can take the same token of value, copy it, and give it to you, somebody else, and a dozen other people. This has the effect of infinitely inflating the supply, which is ruinous to any system of money. My ability to send the same unit of currency to multiple people by copying it is known as the "double-spend problem," and it has tormented digital money developers for decades.

At first glance it may appear that banks face a similar problem. After all, every time someone sends money through the banking system via check or credit card or other electronic transaction the banks are dealing with what are in essence "digital dollars." However, banks have solved the double-spend program by functioning as the trusted third party that performs the action of debiting your account and crediting my account when you pay me. As noted above, the central banks may not be trustworthy in terms of sufficiently limiting the money supply, but the overall banking system does a decent job of keeping track of the dollars that move through the system and preventing anyone from sending the same dollar to any recipient that they already sent to someone else.

This is something that no electronic money developer was able to achieve until Bitcoin arrived. Bitcoin is the first electronic system of money to solve the trusted third-party problem that frustrated the Internet money developers for so long. It did this by distributing trust among multiple parties. It created a system in which (1) everyone in the Bitcoin network can maintain a copy of the ledger, and (2) there are *economic incentives* for the network participants to avoid cheating the system. Let's examine how this brilliant system works.

The Bitcoin network is an Internet-native system of money. It is open, permission-less, decentralized, peer-to-peer, and distributed. It allows the participation of anyone who runs the network's open-source software protocol. Each node in the network maintains a copy of the entire transaction history, including the creation and transfer of every single bitcoin[1] since the network's inception. This ledger of who owned what in the past and who owns what now is akin to a worldwide bank that maintains a ledger with different bank accounts and amounts for each of its account holders.

There are some important differences between such a bank system and the Bitcoin network, however. The first difference is that in the Bitcoin network, every node operator keeps a copy of the ledger and can verify its accuracy. This prevents any single third party from controlling the network.

The second difference is that being an "account holder" is not directly tied to identity; it is only defined by possession of a password known as a "private key." The private key is held by the owner of the bitcoins, and it is uniquely associated with an "address" on the ledger that functions like an account number. If I want to send bitcoins to you, you give me your address, and I use my private key linked with my address to send the payment to your address. You can subsequently use your private key to send bitcoins from your address to someone else. So far so good, but there is a major problem. What if I attempt to send the same bitcoins to two different people? This double-spend problem discussed earlier was unsolved until Bitcoin.

Cryptography 101

To proceed further it's helpful to explain some of the basic technological building blocks that Bitcoin uses. The cryptographic technology for the pairing of private keys with addresses described earlier is based on "public key cryptography." Specifically, Bitcoin uses the Elliptic Curve Digital Signature Algorithm (ECDSA).[90] Like other cryptographic tools, ECDSA is known as a

---

1 I will try to observe the industry convention, which is to capitalize Bitcoin when referring to the overall network, but not capitalizing it when referring to the unit of account. For example: "I send you a bitcoin by using the Bitcoin network."

"one-way function." This is a mathematical operation whereby, given an output of the function, it's easy to check if a given input is the correct input, but very hard to find the input if you don't know it already. In other words, it's easy to check if your "private key" fits the "lock," but if you don't already have the key, it's very hard to find such a key. The only known way to solve for the input for such a function is by brute force calculation.

To illustrate the point, imagine you are faced with a very secure door lock and you have access to a pile of keys. You know one of them fits the lock, so all you have to do is try them all by hand. Now imagine that the pile of keys is the size of the Milky Way Galaxy. Trying them all by hand might take you longer than the life of the universe. Today and for the foreseeable future, the computational resources to solve the ECDSA function for the private key by "brute force" (i.e., by trying all the possible keys) exceed those available to humankind. This may not always be the case if people eventually build powerful quantum computers or if someone discovers a new mathematical way of "solving" the encryption that has eluded cryptographers for decades. However, the history of cryptography has so far demonstrated cryptographers' ability to devise stronger locks before anyone is able to figure out how to "pick" the existing ones.

The cryptographic technology needed to understand the solution to the double-spend problem mentioned earlier is called a hash function. In the case of Bitcoin, the hash function is called Secure Hash Algorithm 256, or SHA-256. Just like ECDSA, which provides people with keys that secure their Bitcoin funds, SHA-256 is a one-way function that makes it easy to calculate whether a given input results in a given output, but very difficult to search for an input that results in a given output if you don't know the input in advance. Like all hash functions, SHA-256 also has some other useful properties. For a given input of any length or complexity, it produces an output of a specific uniform length and complexity. Additionally, small changes in the input result in large and apparently random changes in the output.

To understand how it works, we'll use a simplified example. Let's call our fictional hash function "Sixhash." Sixhash takes any input and outputs a six-digit number. For example, if we input the phrase "Bitcoin is the best form of money," it outputs "729122." If we input "4," it outputs "241236." So we see that two inputs of different length and complexity both result in a six-digit output. What's more interesting is that if we input "5," the output is "785571." So we observe that changing the input from "4" to "5" results in two outputs ("241236" and "785571") that appear unrelated to each other. Numerical relationships between inputs don't reveal relationships between their outputs, and vice versa. SHA-256, the hashing algorithm used in Bitcoin, works the same way, except that the output is a 64-character alphanumeric output. With SHA-256 we observe the following:

If we input "4," the output is:
"4b227777d4dd1fc61c6f884f48641d02b4d121d3fd328cb08b5531fcacdabf8a"

If we input "5," the output is:
"ef2d127de37b942baad06145e54b0c619a1f22327b2ebbcfbec78f5564afe39d"

This level of complexity in the output means that although there is certainly more than one input that will lead to the same output (what's known as a "collision"), the set of possible outputs is so enormous that the computational difficulty of finding two inputs that lead to the same output is extraordinarily high.

Let's return to the double-spend problem mentioned earlier. Here's how Bitcoin solves it. Getting a transaction included in the Bitcoin ledger requires that it be included in a "block" (a set) of transactions. Such a block of transactions occurs when a "miner" (the Bitcoin network's term for a computer that voluntarily joins the network with the intent of processing users' transactions) does the following. It takes all of the transactions broadcast to the network in the last 10 minutes and checks that all the transactions that have been requested by users (such as me sending you a bitcoin) are valid, including (but not limited to) verifying that my address (account) actually has enough bitcoins in it to send the bitcoin to you. Then it runs the transactions through the SHA-256 algorithm. It also calculates a SHA-256 hash of the current time and a SHA-256 hash of the cumulative chain of previous transaction blocks. Finally, it adds up these numbers and attempts to find a number that when summed with those already-calculated variables and collectively run through the SHA-256 hash, results in an output that starts with a certain number of zeros (say twenty). Finding this solution, which includes the legitimate transactions, results in the creation of a valid block of transactions, and this block gets added to the chain of all prior blocks known as the Bitcoin blockchain. This is how Bitcoin's monetary "ledger" is constructed.

To return to our prior analogy of searching through a galaxy-sized stack of keys to find the one that opens the lock, the situation in the last paragraph is akin to trying to open a lock for which a large number of keys will open the lock, but that large number is still much smaller than the available set of possible keys. So perhaps the pile of acceptable keys is the size of a house. That's a lot of possible keys, but still far fewer than the galaxy-sized pile from the prior scenario. We can further modify the analogy and specify that opening the lock actually requires the use of four keys, three of which are clearly specified (the sum of the transactions, the time, and the prior block of transactions mentioned in the prior paragraph) and the fourth is just one of the house-sized pile of keys that must be searched for among the galaxy-sized pile of keys. Finding one of the possible fourth keys that completes the set is computationally difficult because it involves trying random numbers, running them through the SHA-256 hash calculation, and checking to see if the output satisfies the requirement of a number starting with a certain number of zeros. But it's far easier than our earlier brute force computation example, and every 10 minutes on average some lucky miner succeeds in solving this computational problem. Because they are computationally intensive and require lots of mathematical work (and energy), these solutions are called "proof of work."

Since reaching such a computational solution is difficult and comes with a large payoff, it is akin to "striking gold," and is apparently the source of the term "miner" within the Bitcoin system. In exchange for completing this mining process, the winning miner is rewarded with a newly minted set of bitcoins (currently 12.5 bitcoins per 10-minute block of transactions) and also any fees attached to transactions requested by network users (such as me sending you a bitcoin) in order to prioritize their transactions in the queue of pending transactions. Such transaction fees are akin to paying the bouncer at the door of the night club to skip the queue. When lots of people are trying to send transactions simultaneously, the fees rise in a similar manner to "surge pricing" when you're trying to catch a ride with Uber or Lyft.

This mining process allows anyone to commit resources to the network's security in any amount. However, the computational difficulty of "solving" a block of transactions means that it is costly to run mining computers. What has happened in practice is that large industrial data center management operations provide most of the mining capacity because there are economies of scale associated with running computational hardware. Also, in order to spread the compensation and reduce the risk of running computers for long periods of time before getting lucky enough to solve a block and get paid, miners band together into mining "pools" that help them even out their income over time. This is similar to the way groups of people at the office combine their funds to buy a pooled set of lottery tickets and split the winnings.

A Secure, Attack-Resistant Money

The mining process makes double-spending or reversing transactions extraordinarily difficult and expensive. The system therefore achieves a high level of "immutability," and such immutability is what makes Bitcoin such good money. Remember that money is a ledger, which is a record of who owns what amount of the money. Historically, a lot of the ways that money has gone wrong have involved altering the ledger. Thefts (someone illegitimately moving money from your ledger account to theirs), account freezes (someone freezing the balance of your ledger account so you can't use it), and government printing too much money (adding too much to its own ledger account out of thin air and thereby diluting the purchasing power of everyone else's) are all examples of harmful attacks on the monetary ledger. Ledger immutability, except when the money holder consents to a transaction, is fundamental to good money.

The first way mining achieves ledger immutability is the fact that anyone can join the effort to provide network security by mining. Any centralized authority attempting to hijack the system can therefore be counteracted by new participants joining the system. The second way immutability is achieved is through the proof of work mechanism described earlier. The difficulty of proof of work means that miners must purchase specialized computer hardware known as an ASIC (Application-Specific Integrated Circuit). Such hardware is optimized to mine for the Bitcoin network but is useless for anything else. This means that any attacker has to either purchase or co-opt specialized equipment in order to attack the network, and such an investment cannot be recouped or recycled since it is only useful for Bitcoin mining. This expense provides a huge deterrent to attacking the network.

The third way mining achieves immutability is that even if an attacker can marshal enough resources to acquire a large portion of the world's ASIC capacity, attacking the network is costly on an *ongoing* basis. That's because running ASICs requires a lot of electricity, and not only is such energy expenditure expensive, but attacking the network is also likely to reduce the value of the bitcoins that are awarded to the attacker. So the attacker has to acquire expensive specialized equipment, has to use a lot of costly electricity in order to maintain the attack on an ongoing basis, and sees the value of his mining reward in bitcoins fall due to the attack that he himself has launched.

Lastly, a "successful" attack doesn't even accomplish much. It only allows the attacker to (1) refuse to validate legitimate transactions (i.e., block them and thereby mine empty or partially empty transaction blocks), (2) double-spend bitcoins in addresses for which he has the private keys, or (3) if he can muster a majority of the mining power of the entire network, reverse transactions in recent history. We'll examine these categories of attack in greater detail in Chapters 10 and 11.

We have now covered the basics of Bitcoin. In the following two chapters, we'll examine Bitcoin in the context of what we learned in earlier chapters about what makes good money.

Chapter 8

Bitcoin as Money

Bitcoin as Story and Social Consensus

In Chapter 4, we noted that money is a story and a social consensus in a similar way that the Constitution of the United States is. Just as the Constitution lays out the basic principles for the governance of the nation known as the United States, the Bitcoin whitepaper lays out the basic rules underpinning the Bitcoin network.[91] In the U.S., the legislature (Congress) passes laws, the judiciary (courts) interprets them, and the executive (President and subsidiary departments) executes them. Over time this process creates the full and detailed *implementation* of the tenets of the Constitution. Similarly, the Bitcoin open-source software code is the actual implementation of the fundamental tenets of Bitcoin. These basic credos include Bitcoin's openness to users who want to transact or support the network by mining, as well as Bitcoin's limited and clearly defined supply schedule.

Just as amending the Constitution is very difficult, changing the Bitcoin consensus rules (such as the number of bitcoins created with each new block of transactions) has proven extraordinarily difficult. The underlying principles of Bitcoin, which are codified in the code that is run by its thousands of nodes, are continuing to gain an ever-growing body of adherents. Those adherents have come to expect Bitcoin to maintain certain principles, and the social consensus around those principles seems to strengthen with time.

Bitcoin as Protocol

Lots of technologies are protocols. They meet Chapter 4's definition of a protocol as *a set of procedures or rules for acting*, and since Bitcoin is a network, it also meets the network-context protocol definition as a set of procedures or rules for *interacting with each other*. Telephone systems are the textbook example. In the early days of telephone systems, it didn't make much sense for there to be a multitude of different telephone protocol designs because that would have interfered with the ability of everyone to talk to each other. In the United States we therefore ended up with a single company (AT&T) running a single set of telephone system protocols. Even after "Ma Bell" was broken up into different companies, its offshoots continued to use the same protocols.

In the 1960s the U.S. government agency that would later become DARPA (Defense Advanced Research Projects Agency) recognized a national security need to transmit data rapidly and robustly over distance without having to resort to the audio formats provided by the telephone system at that time. The existing telephone protocol, which was the dominant mode of long-distance communication, depended on dedicated links that could be vulnerable to attack. So the new project, dubbed the "ARPANET" (Advanced Research Projects Agency Network) was based on a very different concept: data packet switching. Over time and with lots of development work and funding, these protocols became formalized into what is now known as TCP/IP (Transmission Control Protocol/Internet Protocol).[92] Once a critical mass of Internet service providers adopted TCP/IP and started building higher-level protocols on top of it, a powerful network effect came into play. Almost every new application involving data transmission over distance used TCP/IP, which made more people want to build using TCP/IP since doing so would allow maximum compatibility with the rest of the existing infrastructure.

One of the things built on top of the TCP/IP protocol was another protocol called SMTP (Simple Mail Transfer Protocol). This higher-level protocol comprised a set of standards that enabled email format and transfer. Once

SMTP was adopted by enough email providers (Microsoft's Hotmail, Google's Gmail, etc.), it became embedded and entrenched in the larger Internet ecosystem, just as TCP/IP had done on a lower level.

Like SMTP and others, Bitcoin is a protocol that is built on top of another protocol (TCP/IP). Indeed, venture capitalist Chris Burniske and investor Jack Tatar have aptly labeled it "MOIP," or Money Over Internet Protocol.[93] Most Internet protocols, including TCP/IP and SMTP, are free and open-source. This has allowed capable business organizations (Google, Amazon, Facebook, etc.) to build multi-hundred-billion-dollar enterprises on top of these free protocols by capturing and exploiting customer data, which their customers serve to them for free. Facebook is the classic example. You spend hours uploading your intimate details, and Facebook gets to monetize all your personal data without compensating you, other than giving you a convenient way to communicate online, and without compensating the creators of the free and open-source Internet protocols that make it all possible.

Bitcoin is different in one crucial dimension. With Bitcoin, the major economic value is embedded *in the protocol itself* because the open-source software and data structure that includes people's Bitcoin account balances (i.e., the ledger) are inseparable from each other. So instead of a final application layer above the protocol layer capturing all the value, as has happened with most Internet protocols, with Bitcoin the protocol layer captures significant value. At the time of this writing, that value amounts to roughly $150 billion. Undoubtedly, the companies that build an ecosystem on top of Bitcoin will also create and capture substantial value. That doesn't diminish the fact that Bitcoin is the first open-source Internet protocol to capture significant value and that the amount of value that could potentially accrue to Bitcoin is much, much larger than its current $150 billion. This point is critical to understanding the upside potential of Bitcoin.

One of my favorite technology writers is Andy Kessler. He started his career as an engineer at Bell Labs, an organization that attracted exceptional technical talent and birthed many of the core telecom technologies that undergirded America's phone system. Subsequently, he worked as an analyst on Wall Street, and then ran a tech-focused hedge fund in the 1990s (a very profitable time for such an endeavor).[94] Having made his fortune, he started writing books and articles on the tech space and became a regular on *The Wall*

Street Journal's op-ed page. I have read several of his books, and I regularly read his opinions. He writes great stuff.

So I was surprised to read his August 27, 2017, *Wall Street Journal* op-ed, which said that a bitcoin was only worth about $100.[95] At the time, a bitcoin was trading at around $4,300, or 43x Kessler's estimate of fair value. His argument assumed that Bitcoin was trying to replace Visa and Mastercard, which combined were worth around $377 billion at the time. If Bitcoin were to achieve an equal market capitalization to that of the Visa/Mastercard duopoly, this would have equated to roughly $25,000 per bitcoin. But Kessler argued that because the Bitcoin network charges much lower transaction fees than Visa/Mastercard, applying a similar valuation multiple *on transaction fees* would result in a much lower valuation for Bitcoin than for the Visa/Mastercard duopoly.

The day after reading Kessler's piece I wrote a response, which *The Wall Street Journal* published on September 13, 2017.[96] I pointed out that Bitcoin's value as a payment system was unlikely to be reduced due to its lower fees. Instead, the $377 billion combined Visa/Mastercard market capitalization would likely accrue to Bitcoin, especially due to network effects that are fundamental to money. I also pointed out that today gold isn't used as a medium of exchange, but it is an $8 trillion asset, and that Bitcoin would only need to capture a slice of that to become much more valuable.

Almost two years later, I still believe that this bifurcation between (1) the payments system function (which is comparable to Visa/Mastercard), and (2) the long-serving monetary asset known as gold, provides one of the keys to understanding Bitcoin's potential. Six months after my public exchange with Kessler in *The Wall Street Journal*, Saifedean Ammous published *The Bitcoin Standard* (mentioned in Chapter 2). This book took the analysis to the next level. It included an excellent detailed synthesis of Bitcoin's potential to become a gold-like monetary base layer with "second layer" payment systems (comparable to Visa/Mastercard) built on top of it.

To understand the difference between a base settlement layer and a second payment layer, consider the U.S. dollar. The base layer of the U.S. dollar (what monetary economists call "M0") is the printed cash in circulation: green pieces of paper with denominations of $1, $5, $20, $50 and $100. Structurally, this base layer is analogous to the global stock of gold. An obvious problem with this physical cash base layer is that cash does not transfer easily over distance. Adding a basic banking payments system on top of the base layer, such as the SWIFT system for wire transfers or the ACH for bank-to-bank transfers, solves this long-distance cash transfer problem. This additional payment system represents a "second layer" on top of the first layer. The more recently created smartphone-based peer-to-peer payment systems Venmo (owned by PayPal) and Square Cash (owned by Square) also ably satisfy this need for payment over distance, but today they depend on the second-layer banking system. They therefore represent a *third* layer. The credit card processors like Visa and Mastercard also represent a third layer on top of the second-layer banking system. Most people use credit cards or debit cards issued by banks. Both of these card systems run on payment rails that require the second-layer banking system in order to function.

In the credit card system, consumers get (1) consumer credit, (2) "float" (funds provided to users for free until the next billing statement, assuming the user pays her bill on time), and (3) loyalty rewards (effectively kickbacks paid to the consumer that come out of the merchant's hide). Merchants get some benefit due to the reduction in risk of theft of cash, both by employees running the registers and non-employee robbers wielding weapons. But merchants are generally reluctant participants in the system and in most cases would prefer a world without credit cards. That's because in exchange for this arrangement, the credit card network operators (Visa/Mastercard) and the card-issuing banks together extract a somewhat exorbitant fee of roughly 2%, most of which is effectively paid by the merchants. Moreover, the merchants are often hit with chargebacks and losses to fraud. The card issuers also get the opportunity to charge consumers interest rates on balances carried beyond the free "float" period. Such interest averaged almost 18% annualized as of May 2019.[97] The credit card issuers also get to aggregate customers' spending and payment history and sell it to companies interested in such information.[98]

This system is a wildly profitable business model (for Visa/Mastercard and, to a lesser extent, the card-issuing banks) that looks somewhat like those of the Internet monopolists such as Google and Facebook. The merchants that sell the goods and services in the credit card payment system are analogous to the creators of media content, like newspapers, that Google and Facebook take advantage of. Like media content creators who are forced to reach their audiences via Google and Facebook, the merchants now face an intermediary (the credit card system) that doesn't benefit them but that they effectively pay for. The consumers are slightly better off than they would be otherwise. But the network intermediary (whether Visa/Mastercard or Google/Facebook) gets rich.

Critics of Bitcoin like to talk about transaction throughput—the number of transactions that flow through the system—and they especially like to compare Bitcoin's throughput to that of the credit card system. Today the Bitcoin network's transaction throughput is only about five transactions per second. Visa claims 24,000–65,000 maximum transactions per second.[99,100] I therefore assume that combined Visa/Mastercard transaction capacity is on the order of 100,000 transactions per second. But since Visa/Mastercard is a third layer above the existing payments system, and Bitcoin is a base layer, this comparison is ridiculous. It's a bit like complaining in 1995 that the TCP/IP Internet protocol (essentially a base layer) was no good because it couldn't stream video like cable television could. Less than 20 years later we had high-definition streaming television over the Internet via Netflix. It just took some time for the additional layers to be built that would deliver the dramatically improved data throughput needed to support streaming video.

Today there are already several additional layers being built on Bitcoin. The most developed is the existing set of Bitcoin exchanges and custodians, including Coinbase, Kraken, BitGo, Xapo, and others. These companies allow transfers between accounts similarly to the way the banking system allows transfers of dollars between account holders at the same bank. This system is less secure than settling transactions directly through the Bitcoin network, but it is faster. Another system, which has been built by Bitcoin development organization Blockstream, is called Liquid. It is a "sidechain" that allows large numbers of bitcoins to transfer between exchanges and settles such transactions periodically to the Bitcoin blockchain.

Perhaps the best-known and most promising new layer being built on Bitcoin is the Lightning Network. This system allows users to open and close direct and multi-leg payment channels among participants. It facilitates huge increases in transaction volumes (potentially allowing hundreds of thousands or even millions of transactions per second) by only settling occasionally through the Bitcoin network. It is analogous to the second-layer and third-layer systems that exist on top of the U.S. dollar today. Although it is still in "beta" mode, the Lightning Network is functional, and the amount of software development talent drawn to it seems to be growing quickly.

These various layers being built on top of Bitcoin are well on their way to facilitating volumes of transactions that are multiple orders of magnitude higher than the Bitcoin base layer provides today.

Bitcoin as the Scarcest Money

Bitcoin's scarcity is far better than that of the dollar (or any fiat currency). Among a number of reasons that scarcity of currency matters is the fact that the lack of monetary scarcity, due to central banks printing more of it at will, is one of the key causes of the growing debt that is engulfing the world. As discussed in Chapter 4, a fractional reserve system in which the central bank can create more money and thereby abet deficit spending out of a myopic concern with *consumer price* inflation and a failure to consider the consequences of *asset price* inflation, seems to result in ever-rising debt levels.

A gold standard is better than the dollar in terms of scarcity, but not as good as Bitcoin. The scarcity of gold makes creating money more difficult than with the dollar, but new gold supply can still be extracted from the earth at a rate of 1%–2% annually. Gold also disappoints users by being much harder to transfer than fiat currency, especially over long distances. A paper-based gold standard (in which paper notes are backed by gold held in vaults) solves the transferability problem. However, history shows that governments are unable to adhere to a gold standard because the temptation to take advantage of the stealth tax known as seigniorage (printing valuable money at low cost) is too great.

Bitcoin, in contrast to the dollar, to gold, and to any other currency in the history of the world, is the hardest money ever invented—"hard" being the word international currency analysts, economists, and traders use to describe money that is *hard to produce* and therefore scarce. Its predetermined cap of 21 million bitcoins operates on a supply schedule as follows. The Bitcoin network validates a block of transactions approximately every 10 minutes, and a set of new bitcoins is minted as a "block subsidy" with each such block. Every 210,000 blocks (which equates to approximately four years), the number of new bitcoins minted for each block subsidy falls by 50%. For the first four years of Bitcoin's existence, 50 new bitcoins were awarded with each new block. For the next four years, 25 bitcoins were. Currently 12.5 bitcoins are minted with every 10-minute transaction block, and in mid-2020 it will fall to 6.25 bitcoins per block. The supply schedule and the implied inflation rate for Bitcoin's first 20 years is shown in Figure 7:

Figure 7: Supply Schedule and Implied Inflation Rate for Bitcoin's First 20 Years

Year #	Year	Bitcoins Minted per Block	Bitcoins Minted	Total Bitcoins in Existence	Annual Inflation	
1	2009	50	2,628,000	2,628,000		
2	2010	50	2,628,000	5,256,000	100.00%	
3	2011	50	2,628,000	7,884,000	50.00%	
4	2012	50	2,628,000	10,512,000	33.33%	
5	2013	25	1,314,000	11,826,000	12.50%	
6	2014	25	1,314,000	13,140,000	11.11%	
7	2015	25	1,314,000	14,454,000	10.00%	
8	2016	25	1,314,000	15,768,000	9.09%	
9	2017	12.5	657,000	16,425,000	4.17%	
10	2018	12.5	657,000	17,082,000	4.00%	
11	2019	12.5	657,000	17,739,000	3.85%	<-- We are here
12	2020	12.5	657,000	18,396,000	3.70%	
13	2021	6.25	328,500	18,724,500	1.79%	
14	2022	6.25	328,500	19,053,000	1.75%	
15	2023	6.25	328,500	19,381,500	1.72%	
16	2024	6.25	328,500	19,710,000	1.69%	
17	2025	3.125	164,250	19,874,250	0.83%	
18	2026	3.125	164,250	20,038,500	0.83%	
19	2027	3.125	164,250	20,202,750	0.82%	
20	2028	3.125	164,250	20,367,000	0.81%	

The next "halving" of the block subsidy is projected to occur in 2020, and this event will reduce the annual inflation from 3.70% to 1.79%. This will make Bitcoin's annual supply inflation approximately equal to that of gold, and is the reason Bitcoin has earned the moniker "digital gold." Another four years later, Bitcoin's annual supply inflation will be reduced to approximately half that of gold, and it will continue falling until it reaches zero in the year 2140, assuming 10-minute average block times.

Returning briefly to the gold market, a higher gold price allows gold mines that were unprofitable at lower gold prices to become profitable. This means that an increase in demand for gold, which cause an increase in the price of gold, results in an increase in gold supply as more gold miners come online. Bitcoin doesn't work this way. Instead, the appearance of additional mining (network transaction validation node) capacity increases the difficulty of the hashing algorithm discussed earlier in this chapter such that the creation rate of new bitcoins continues to follow the predetermined schedule. Rather than the rate of supply of bitcoins increasing, the network's *security* increases. This characteristic of adjusting the mining difficulty in order to maintain the predictable supply of new bitcoins is one of the system's key features.

While it's important to have access to some money that is unseizable and censorship-resistant (characteristics we'll discuss later), Bitcoin's status as the world's hardest (scarcest) money is likely to be the most important factor in its long-term success. In Chapter 5, I suggested that the path the Federal Reserve and other central banks will choose out of the debt morass will likely include redistribution, financial repression (lowering interest rates below zero), and inflation. Suppose that in the next recession the Federal Reserve and other central banks lower short-term interest rates below zero, such that your checking account pays you *negative* 1% annually. This means that $1,000 left in your checking account shrinks to $990 by the end of the year. Will you draw all your money out as physical cash and stash it under your mattress? Probably not. That's because then you would have to worry about the security of that physical cash, and you would also forego the ability to write checks and pay people remotely.

Now suppose that *two* recessions from now, the Federal Reserve and other central banks lower short-term interest rates to negative 5%. At that level of financial repression, you might strongly consider the cash-under-the-mattress option. But what if the Federal Reserve stops printing physical cash? There are serious policy experts, such as Harvard economist Ken Rogoff, who advocate getting rid of cash completely.[101] Countries like China and Sweden have mostly done away with it already. Interestingly, some countries have resisted the trend. Germany has maintained a high level of physical cash usage, possibly due to its bad experience with totalitarianism.[102]

But now the world has an alternative: Bitcoin. This money is effectively cash, but you don't have to physically put it under your mattress. Instead, you can memorize your private key or memorize some mnemonics that allow you to access the key, or write the key down and split it into pieces that you hide in different places. You can layer on additional protections such as systems that require participation from some minimum number of parties (say two out of three, or three out of five) or encryption of the keys themselves. The possibilities are manifold.

Additionally, because the Bitcoin supply is strictly limited, it is likely to increase in value over time as the economy grows, rather than losing 5% a year if interest rates go deeply negative. After it reaches maturity with a value in the trillions or tens of trillions of dollars, its value will probably grow at a rate similar to that of global GDP. Which form of money will you choose: the one that loses 5% of its value annually, or the one that maintains or gains value over time?

Critics point out that anyone can create a cryptocurrency, which implies that no cryptocurrency (including Bitcoin) is scarce. But as we learned in Chapter 6, money is a protocol with network effects. So far, no cryptocurrency's network effect comes close to Bitcoin's. Starting a competing cryptocurrency at this point is similar to starting a new social network to compete with Facebook. Such an effort will have a very low probability of success. We will return to this theme in Chapter 11 when we explore competitive risks to Bitcoin.

Bitcoin as the Most Unseizable Money ("Leggo my Crypto!")

Ask an upper-middle-class liberal American how much she cares about unseizability. You may be met with a blank stare. Next ask a Ukrainian, Cypriot, Indian, or Syrian who has lived through a mass asset confiscation in the last decade. Or ask a Chinese citizen if he would like to be able to store some hard-earned cash out of the physical reach of the government. Or ask your Jewish friend about whether her grandparents would have liked to have had access to a form of money that they could have carried out of Nazi Germany just by remembering a password. It's possible that the passage of time has reduced the salience of this scenario for her. But it's probably top-of-mind to a Venezuelan refugee today.

Like home insurance, the safety provided by unseizability is something that you probably don't need. Until you do. And when you do, you *really* do. This illustrates the potential for differences in preferences for different kinds of money among different people. Furthermore, although one person may have a general preference for a certain form of money that scores highly along certain parameters, she might not want that form of money to account for 100% of her personal portfolio of money. She might want to hold some amount of a form that may be more useful in certain circumstances. She might want to hold some quantity of gold or bitcoins for a "rainy day."

Consider the following recent example. On November 8, 2016, India's government declared that all 500-rupee and 1,000-rupee notes could no longer be used in shops.[103] These notes accounted for approximately 86% of all cash in circulation in the country. Indian citizens were given seven weeks to trade their existing notes for new ones. The stated reason for the shock was to crack down on corruption. The idea was that people who had accumulated large amounts of cash without paying tax would be forced to submit their now-obsolete notes and thereby illuminate their tax evasion.

Unfortunately, the distribution of the new cash was bungled, and it had an adverse effect on the Indian economy.[104] As usual with failed economic policy, the poorest were probably the ones who suffered the most. India is a cash-based economy, especially in rural areas that are poorest. Two months after the event, reports suggested that nearly 15 trillion rupees of the 15.4 trillion total rupees taken out of circulation were accounted for. So either the rich weren't hoarding as much untaxed money as was supposed, or they were successful in laundering it. If you were a rich Indian tax evader, you might have used the seven-week window to contact some poor Indians and offer them a 5% "fee" to take your cash to the bank and trade it for the new cash. Although this would result in zero additional tax revenue for the government, it would at least be somewhat redistributive since most of your cash mules would probably be poor. Unfortunately, it would also turn them into criminals.

You might expect this sort of monetary mayhem in a dictatorship. But India is a representative democracy with a nominally independent central bank.

Admittedly, India's democratic history is not nearly as long as that of the United States, and it has not had as much time to develop its institutions as many western countries have. Nevertheless, this story should give pause to anyone who is too confident that government is going to "do the right thing" with respect to monetary management.

That brings us to the United States. How much do you trust your government to do the right thing? For me, the answer is 75%. I trust my government to treat me fairly 75% of the time. Everyone's answer will be different, but if you answered anything less than 100%, you are in the majority.

Figure 8 shows the trend of trust in government in the United States over the last 60 years through 2017, according to Pew Research.[105] It's currently near the lowest it has ever been, and although it is cyclical, the long-term trend is clearly downward. If you are in the 80%+ majority and don't trust your government "always or most of the time," you might seriously consider forms of money other than the U.S. dollar, such as Bitcoin.

Bitcoin as the World's Most Accessible Money

On the morning of September 11, 2001, I was just waking up when my girlfriend's best friend knocked loudly on the door. "The World Trade Center was hit by an airplane!" she yelled. I'm sometimes reminded of my immediate reply through the door: "Well, what do you want me to do about it?" In my defense, it wasn't yet clear what tragedy had befallen the World Trade Center, its occupants, and surrounding structures and people that day. I don't think I'd even heard of the World Trade Center, much less had any concept of its physical size or psychological importance. But certainly I had no concept of the vast economic, societal, or geopolitical changes this event would set in motion.

Figure 8: Trend of Trust in United States Government

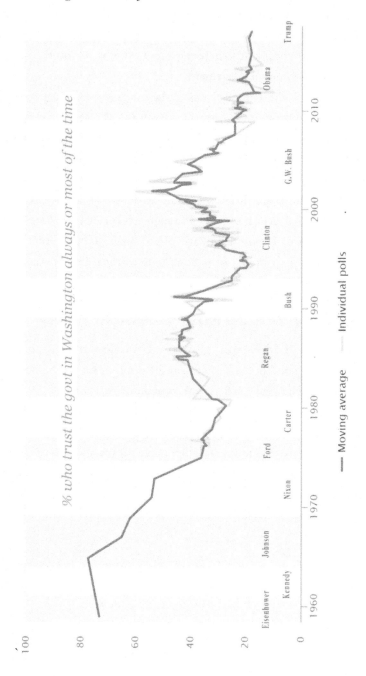

Source: Pew Research

The total number of Americans killed in terrorist acts, including the September 11 attacks, is approximately 3,000 people.[106] Additionally, approximately 43,000 health problems have been attributed to the attack, including thousands of cancer cases.[107] The loss of life and health is a terrible tragedy. In the aftermath of the attacks, Congress and the President enacted far-reaching laws and policies that still touch many facets of society in the United States and abroad. Of course the most dramatic were the actions taken by U.S. military forces and intelligence agencies associated with the wars in Iraq and Afghanistan. These actions caused unquantifiable suffering. They cost thousands of American lives and hundreds of thousands of foreign lives.[108] They also cost trillions of dollars of American treasure.[109]

Another hugely impactful result of the September 11 attacks was the Patriot Act.[110] I say impactful not because it has deterred money laundering or terrorist finance, but because it has probably excluded hundreds of millions of people from the global banking system. Today, over 80% of adults on earth have cell phones. They can communicate with the rest of the world with the push of a few buttons. Yet according to the United Nations Department of Economic and Social Affairs, two billion people globally do not have access to a bank account.[111] How did we end up with this bizarre outcome?

According to an FDIC report, roughly 8.4 million households representing 20.5 million people in the United States were "unbanked" in 2017.[112] This is a significant problem for these Americans since it's more expensive and dangerous to operate outside the banking system. But the human cost associated with the number of people who do not have access to safe and dependable money transmission mechanisms is far greater in poorer countries.

I attribute much of this "financial exclusion" problem to the Patriot Act and the now-prevailing regulatory system for global banking. The Patriot Act saddled banks based in the United States and Europe with much higher potential liability resulting from activities thought to be linked to terrorism in all their branches, including in poor countries, and even from activities in *third-party* banks located in those countries that touch them or transfer money to them. Since people in poor countries have less money than in rich countries like the United States, opening a bank in a poor country is already a less-profitable business opportunity unless you charge your customers more (as a percentage) for the service than you would in a rich country. Add on potential liability from money laundering and terrorism that any international correspondent bank takes on, and it's no wonder that two billion people around the world have been unable to find a bank willing to serve them.

Now consider the imbalance in the costs and benefits of these antiterrorism efforts. Following is a cost/benefit analysis that reduces the potential for human tragedy to a number. This may offend some readers, but tragic as the results of the World Trade Center attack were for the thousands of people killed, and tragic as the loss of life from any additional terrorist attacks would be, it's also important to examine the Patriot Act's far-reaching effects on millions of people in places far from the attack.

It is impossible to know how many American lives would have been lost without the new rules that resulted from the September 11 attacks, but I suspect it is hundreds or possibly thousands, so I'm going to estimate 5,000. This assumes there would have been another attack with direct deaths somewhat larger in number than the September 11 attacks. It's also impossible to know how many people have been excluded from the global financial system as a direct result of the Patriot Act, but I suspect it is in the hundreds of millions. If we assume that 5,000 Americans would have died in additional terrorist attacks if the Patriot Act hadn't been implemented, and if we further assume that 500 million people would have been able to gain financial access to the global banking system if the Patriot Act hadn't been implemented, then we infer a ratio of financial system access loss to lives saved on the order of a *hundred thousand to one.*

It's worth asking whether denying perhaps a hundred thousand people banking access in order to save one American life is a reasonable tradeoff. Because the major banks aren't willing to take on the risk of terrorism prosecution for low-profit customers (and partly because such customers lack reliable identification), hundreds of millions of people are stuck using cash while living and working in some of the world's most dangerous areas. Denial of access to financial services is not just an inconvenience for these people and their families. Because of the risk of mugging and theft, it is a matter of personal safety.

Admittedly, these numbers—of lives saved by the Patriot Act, and of people denied access to the banking system because of it—are unmeasurable and unknowable. But the estimate that an additional 500 million people would by now have gained banking access if not for the Patriot Act is probably con-servative. Remember that when the Patriot Act took effect in 2001, the smartphone hadn't yet been invented, and global Internet penetration was 10%–11%.[113,114] Global Internet penetration has quintupled since then, and the Internet is the best banking tool for most people. How many of these un-banked people would by now have been able to raise their families up from poverty if they'd had access to basic financial tools? How many now-disenfranchised young people would have been able to resist the siren songs of extremism and terrorism?

Moreover, the foregoing calculation doesn't even account for the billions of dollars of annual Patriot Act compliance costs for banks that are a pure tax on the global economy. In May 2019 *The Economist* reported that bank disclosures suggest that roughly 10% of employees at large banks work in compliance, and that this percentage has approximately doubled since the mid-2000s (i.e., since the period soon after the Patriot Act came into effect).[115] As of 2018 the top 15 banks in the U.S. employed roughly 1.1 million people.[116] Excluding Russian banks, the top 15 European banks employed over 1.8 million people in 2017.[117] Using *The Economist's* 10% figure for employees working in compli-ance, the total for the U.S. and Europe excluding Russia would be roughly 290,000 people. Assuming an average salary plus healthcare benefit of $80,000 annually (though it's probably significantly higher), this amounts to salary plus healthcare cost of $23 billion annually for compliance. This doesn't include the cost of office space or technology spending for these people. Perhaps only a fraction of their efforts is dedicated to combatting money-laundering. But the bottom line is that the cost of any incremental protection these rules have may have provided still amounts to billions of dollars and possibly tens of billions of dollars annually.

I would take some solace in this state of affairs if money laundering had been reduced to modest levels. Unfortunately, recent history is not very en-couraging. Following are a few of the scandals that occurred subsequent to the enactment of the Patriot Act. In late 2012, *The New York Times* reported that HSBC had agreed to pay $1.9 billion in fines to settle charges that it had laundered billions of dollars for Mexican drug cartels.[118] Regarding this case the U.S. Justice Department reported that, "In order to efficiently move this volume of cash through the teller windows at HSBC Mexico branches, drug traffickers had designed specially shaped boxes that fit the precise dimensions of the teller windows."[119] In June 2014 the U.S. Department of Justice announced a guilty plea by French bank BNP Paribas and an agreement by the bank to pay $8.9 billion in fines for processing billions of dollars of transactions on behalf of entities and countries subject to sanctions.[120] In February 2018 CNN reported that Rabobank had been fined $369 million for facilitating the laundering of hundreds of millions of dollars in California.[121] In April 2019 *The Guardian* reported that British bank Standard Chartered had been ordered by American and British authorities to pay $1.1 billion in fines for money laundering and sanctions violations.[122]

The money laundering news became truly jaw-dropping in November 2018 when major news outlets reported that roughly €200 billion (equivalent to roughly *$250 billion*) had been laundered through a *single branch* of Denmark's largest bank, Danske Bank, over an eight-year period.[123] Then in March 2019 *The Wall Street Journal* reported that the CEO of Swedbank had been ousted as a result of an investigation into the laundering of "billions" of dollars through the bank.[124] While the total amount of laundering through Swedbank has not yet been disclosed, the case serves as yet another marker on the long and winding road of multi-hundred-billion-dollar laundering schemes enabled by the existing international banking system. The amounts laundered in these schemes dwarf the total of the *entire Bitcoin network* today.

The foregoing list of cases is not comprehensive, as I only spent about an hour searching on Google to fill in the gaps between the cases I knew off the top of my head. Undoubtedly there have been more, and the settled cases are just the tip of the money laundering iceberg because they account for only those perpetrators who *actually get caught*. While it's impossible to estimate with much accuracy, the United Nations office on Drugs and Crime estimates the global money laundering total to be somewhere between $800 billion and $2 *trillion* annually.[125]

In a world where money laundering still occurs on the scale of trillions of dollars a year, and a couple of billion people are still unbanked, it's easy to see the appeal of Bitcoin. Because it allows users to circumvent the banking system from which they have been excluded, Bitcoin could be a great boon to many people, especially in poor countries where the local currency is the least dependable, and where financial access is most scarce. The cost in human misery of the existing systematic exclusion of billions of people from the banking system is immense. Economists and other people have already credited Bitcoin with saving their families from the dire economic consequences of violent and corrupt governments, such as that of Venezuela.[126]

Could a Bitcoin-based system be *worse* than what we have now? I suppose it's possible. But the burden of proof that a Bitcoin-based system that could provide financial access to billions of people would result in *even more* money laundering and criminal activity than the existing system rests on the defenders of the existing system, not on the "revolutionary" supporters of Bitcoin.

Bitcoin as Money that Enables Brand New Uses

Like the new technologies of other eras, and specifically like earlier phases of the Internet, Bitcoin has the potential to serve many more purposes beyond its current applications. The smartphone (which like Bitcoin is Internet-enabled) provides a good example of the way a technology develops over time. Early skeptics of the iPhone criticized it for not being a better phone than existing mobile phones (true) and for being a worse computer than a laptop or desktop (also true). But the iPhone wasn't about just providing a better phone or computer and taking market share from existing phone and computer businesses. It was about creating an easy-to-use mobile device that enabled entirely new applications such as real-time geolocation and traffic-based mapping (Google Maps/Waze), text communication via social networks (Twitter) on-the-go peer-to-peer video communication (FaceTime), high-resolution photography anywhere/anytime (12-megapixel camera), and 24-7 on-demand taxi service (Uber and Lyft). Many of these functions came from outside applications that were served up through the new device. These were new "use cases" that weren't possible before. In this way, the iPhone became a "platform" that enabled entirely new capabilities. Bitcoin is no different. Bitcoin in its current manifestation already competes for a share of the world's gold, fiat currency, and offshore asset markets. These total markets are worth tens of trillions of dollars. But there are also potential uses for Bitcoin that extend beyond these obvious multi-trillion-dollar core areas.

An obvious candidate for "useful thing that money has never been able to do until Bitcoin" is micropayments. One of the optimistic views of the early

Internet builders was that as the Internet made accessing information more useful, it would also be possible to charge small amounts of money in exchange for information. This might provide a new model for content providers (such as journalists) to be paid for their content by a much wider audience of readers. In this way people might be able to buy individual articles for pennies, rather than having to pay more for content that was bundled with other content that they weren't interested in. Had such as system emerged earlier, the Internet might not be so dominated by advertising-dependent information aggregation platforms, such as Facebook and Google.

Unfortunately, micropayments never materialized in the United States apparently because the Visa/Mastercard payment duopoly continues to impose such high minimum charges per transaction that payments of a few cents per article are not feasible. Bitcoin software developers are breaking this barrier. They are currently developing software layers on top of Bitcoin, such as the Lightning Network, that allow payments of less than a penny. This system is still in development and may be a few years away from broad adoption, but it seems to have momentum.

Another obvious use for Bitcoin is remittances. Every week millions of people in America, Britain, Germany, and other western countries take their hard-earned paycheck, travel (often on foot) to their bank or check-cashing establishment, wait in line, and cash their check. Then they travel to the nearest Western Union branch, wait in line, and send a remittance payment to their loved ones in their country of origin. The recipients must then travel to their local branch to pick up the cash. For the privilege of traveling and standing in line to transfer these funds to their loved ones, these workers are charged 7% of the value or more, depending on the receiving country. A capitalist might call this an attractive business. A humanitarian might call it highway robbery. Either way, the global diaspora encompasses hundreds of millions of people, and global remittances exceed $500 billion annually.[127,128] What if people could instead use their mobile phones to send funds in transfers that settle in minutes for fees of less than 1%? Bitcoin offers this potential.

The pursuit of a Bitcoin-based international remittance system has already yielded something potentially even bigger. This story is still being written, but the early chapters are promising. One of the most capable entrepreneurs in the Bitcoin ecosystem is Bill Barhydt, who may have the perfect resume for making waves in Bitcoin. Early in his career, Barhydt worked as a cryptographer at the National Security Agency (NSA), the world's leader in governmental use of cryptography. Later, he worked at Netscape, the first commercially successful Internet browser, which was founded by Marc Andreessen. Subsequently, Barhydt learned about the workings of the financial markets as a quantitative analyst at Goldman Sachs. In September 2014 he founded "ABRA" with the goal of creating A Better Remittance Application to solve the problem described in the prior paragraph. But in late 2017, ABRA launched something even bigger.[129]

ABRA now operates the world's first noncustodial Bitcoin-based investment platform that provides users *anywhere in the world* with exposure to a wide range of assets without having a brokerage account.[130] Here's how it works. The user downloads the ABRA app on her smartphone and funds her ABRA account with fiat money. ABRA takes the fiat money and credits the user's account with bitcoins. The user can then buy any combination of a wide range of fiat currencies, cryptocurrencies, commodities, stocks, or ETFs (exchange-traded funds). When the user makes a purchase of Apple stock, ABRA leaves the bitcoins in the user's possession (literally with a private key on the user's phone and a second key held by ABRA), and then simultaneously takes a short position in bitcoins and a long position in Apple stock on behalf of the user. This gives the user synthetic exposure to Apple stock without ever having to open a brokerage account.

According to Barhydt and his legal team, the system complies with all relevant regulations globally primarily because the user retains possession of a private key, which means that ABRA is not the effective custodian of the funds. Holding the private key is effectively the same as holding the assets, and the user holds the key. Undoubtedly regulators across the world will probe this system's legal compliance, and only time will tell if ABRA's back-end system for swapping bitcoins for other assets is robust and safe. But if the system works, it will represent the first global trade and settlement system allowing people in non-western countries to easily access the world's major liquid assets. This could unlock a giant pool of investment capital and dramatically increase global "financial inclusion," while simultaneously creating significant net new demand for bitcoins.

The Internet has already brought amazing things to billions of people. But up to this point several important components have remained missing. In addition to money (prior to Bitcoin) another major missing component has been *identity and associated personal data security.* Whenever you log in to a website you are forced to manage a password and remember answers to strange personal questions like "what was your first car?" and "at what school did you complete sixth grade?" If you forget your password, then you have to use your email account to reset your password. The result of this system is that your personal information, and therefore your identity, lives in the computer systems of dozens of organizations including branches of government, companies, and nonprofit organizations.

Every one of these systems is a target for identify thieves, and it seems that barely a month goes by without a major identity theft or data breach, such as those that have afflicted retailer Target (70 million identities stolen),[131] U.S. federal government department the Office of Personnel Management (21 million identities stolen),[132] Yahoo! (more than 1 *billion* identities stolen),[133] Marriott International (500 million identities stolen),[134] and Equifax (143 million identities stolen).[135] Forensic analysis of data penetrations is difficult, but the bottom line is that billions of pieces of personal identity information have been stolen.

This system would be much more secure if you could keep personal data on your own encrypted device and use a private key (the kind used to send Bitcoin transactions) to validate your identity. Then hackers would have to hack *each individual's device* rather than just hacking one centralized honeypot and walking away with tens or hundreds of millions of identities. Given how important private key management is to using Bitcoin, its gradual adoption is likely to be a catalyst for people's understanding of how such a private key–based system would work and may therefore accelerate the development of identity security. I hope that a decade from now management of private keys will be both (1) a core life skill, and (2) easy to do because smart developers and entrepreneurs have brought to market "dead simple" private key management services.

Fortunately, smart developers at one company are already building out decentralized identity ("DID") solutions to solve the identity management problem. On May 13, 2019, Microsoft announced that it is building a decentralized identity solution called Identity Overlay Network ("ION").[136] For me, the most interesting part of the announcement was that this new DID system would be secured by the Bitcoin network. While this DID system is nascent, it's hard to overstate the importance of the world's most valuable public company deciding to build on top of Bitcoin.

The aforementioned uses for the Bitcoin network (micropayments system, international remittances, global trading and settlement network for investment assets, and secure decentralized identity) are just a few of a much longer list of applications that thousands of entrepreneurs and software developers are currently building. And these are just the things that people have thought of so far. As with many technologies throughout history, some of the most interesting uses of the Bitcoin technology probably haven't even been imagined yet.

Bitcoin as the Most Transparent Money

Anyone and everyone can examine the Bitcoin blockchain, which contains every transaction ever completed. Anyone can run a full node, which validates the entire transaction history and validates every new 10-minute block of transactions to make sure every transaction is valid. If you were to fall asleep for a year and come back to the system, you could fire up a node, download the entire blockchain in a matter of hours, and synchronize with the network from anywhere in the world via an Internet connection.

The fact that Bitcoin's supply schedule is predetermined and known to all makes it the most transparent and honest money ever created. While gold's mining history gives me some confidence that the gold market won't be hit by a supply shock, I can't be sure of how much gold is accessible in the Earth's crust. I especially can't be sure of how much new supply will arrive once people start mining asteroids.[137] Fiat currencies are even worse. Their supplies are set by a small group of central bankers behind closed doors. In a world where my fiat money steals from my every day as its value is debased due to ongoing printing and ever-falling interest rates, I find comfort in a form of money that resists such debasement.

Bitcoin as the Monetary Apex Predator

Early Bitcoin adopter Dan Held may have best articulated Bitcoin's potential long-term behavior as the "apex predator" of money.[138] All markets for all goods (whether monetary, capital, or consumer) are competitive. This competition drives wealth creation in modern economies. The best market solutions demonstrate their strength, take resources from the weak, and create wealth overall in the process Joseph Schumpeter dubbed "creative destruction."[139] This process mirrors Darwin's competitive "natural selection" that results in the fittest organisms taking shares of their environment away from weaker competitors in nature.[140]

As it is with companies and profit-seeking enterprises, so it is with forms of money. In the next section we will score Bitcoin on the 14 Characteristics of Good Money to help demonstrate why Bitcoin may very well be the "fittest" monetary organism and therefore has a good chance of out-competing other forms of money to achieve a dominant position in the monetary environment.

Bitcoin and the 14 Characteristics of Good Money

In Chapter 6 we examined two major currencies of the last century, the dollar and gold, and scored them on the 14 Characteristics of Good Money. Let's now apply the same scoring system to Bitcoin. In a number of instances, we will give Bitcoin two scores: one based on its current manifestation, and another based on the direction it is moving. Remember, Bitcoin is a young technology, and countless brilliant technologists are currently working day and night around the world to improve it.

1. Identifiable. 5 out of 5. Since a distributed system of computers keeps the Bitcoin ledger, and since access to Bitcoin addresses uses proven cryptographic tools, there is almost no chance that the multiple nodes and miners will fail to distinguish a "fake" bitcoin from a real one.

2. Transferable. 3 out of 5 today, but probably 5 out of 5 in the future. Bitcoin can be sent anywhere in the world in minutes. The "wallets" (software and hardware used to manage private keys) are still a pain to use, but they are improving as numerous organizations launch better products. Some of these groups are large corporations; others are nonprofit hacker teams. Bitcoin transaction fees are currently low (less than a dollar), although in late 2017 they peaked as high as $60. As second-layer protocols, such as the Lightning Network, are built on top of the existing Bitcoin base layer, fees should be kept under control and may even fall to fractions of pennies per transaction at the second layer.

3. Durable. 4 out of 5. Bitcoin's ledger exists on tens of thousands of computers worldwide. If the global Internet goes down, then Bitcoin won't work. But that is a very low-probability outcome because of how the Internet is structured and how much critical infrastructure is built on the Internet. If it does happen, we'll have much larger problems than the loss of Bitcoin, considering how much of global commerce and even healthcare now lives on servers in the "cloud."

4. Divisible. 5 out of 5. Each single bitcoin is divisible to eight decimal places, meaning that each bitcoin is divisible into 100 million pieces, each of which is colloquially known as a "satoshi" or "sat" (in homage to Bitcoin's pseudonymous creator, Satoshi Nakamoto). Even if Bitcoin manages to reach a price of $1 million per bitcoin (over 100x its current price), the smallest denomination (one one-hundred-millionth) of a bitcoin will still be worth only one cent. This can make it highly serviceable for micropayments, as we will discuss later.

5. Dense. 5 out of 5. Bitcoin is the densest form of money in existence. Billions of dollars can be stored on a single piece of paper or USB-sized device.

6. Scarce. 5 out of 5. As we have discussed, scarcity is among the most important of the 14 Characteristics of Good Money. Bitcoin's supply curve is strictly limited to a hard cap of 21 million bitcoins. This limit makes Bitcoin the scarcest money every created.

7. Fungible. 3 out of 5 today, but probably 4 out of 5 in the future. So far, it has usually been the case that a bitcoin is a bitcoin is a bitcoin. However, there have been cases of Bitcoin addresses being blacklisted by governments.

Smart software developers and entrepreneurs are working on solutions for improvements in fungibility. See also the "Private" section later.

8. Short-Term Stable Value. 1 out of 5 today, but probably 3 out of 5 in the future. Bitcoin's price routinely moves by several percentage points daily and occasionally by more than 10% in a day. But the volatility has decreased over the years, and most of the volatility has been upward (i.e., the good kind of volatility). Over time, its maturation will continue to reduce the volatility. However, because the supply of bitcoins is strictly fixed, it will always be true that any change in demand will cause a change in price. There is no supply "cushion" for changes in demand. Therefore, Bitcoin's purchasing power may always fluctuate more than gold's, since gold's supply does respond somewhat to increases in price. In a "hyperbitcoinization" scenario in which Bitcoin takes much of the market share from global fiat currencies and gold, Bitcoin's sheer size might eventually make its purchasing power less volatile than other forms of money. But to achieve volatility lower than gold or the dollar, Bitcoin might have to reach tens of trillions of value (in today's dollars).

9. Long-Term Stable Value. 3 out of 5 today, but probably 5 out of 5 in the future. Because it is a noninflationary asset, Bitcoin should maintain or increase its purchasing power over time. There have been one-year periods in its history when it has lost 80% of its value. But over multi-year time periods, as adoption has increased, Bitcoin's value has increased dramatically. Gold has held its purchasing power over millennia. Since Bitcoin's supply is even more limited than gold's, Bitcoin will probably enjoy rising purchasing power in the long run.

10. Unseizable. 4 out of 5. Except by torture or extortion, Bitcoin is nearly impossible to seize because possession can be protected as long as the holder can remember a password.

11. Censorship-Resistant. 4 out of 5. The design of the Bitcoin network makes it very difficult to stop someone from making a payment. If you can access the Internet, you can pay someone with Bitcoin. Anyone with any fear of being cut off from the financial system, whether via due process, accidental miscarriage of justice, or whim of a malevolent government agent, might want to hold some bitcoins.

12. Private. 2 out of 5 today, but probably 3 out of 5 in the future. The Bitcoin blockchain is fully auditable, so if you're seeking to engage in criminal activity, I don't recommend using Bitcoin. Every transaction can be associated with a particular address. Keys can be generated anonymously, but if someone can link an identity to any transaction into or out of the address, then they have a good chance of identifying the address owner since all transactions to or from the address are visible to the public. Today, companies such as Chainalysis are dedicated to putting these pieces together to monitor the Bitcoin network. Moreover, anyone who buys bitcoins through an exchange such as Coinbase that does "know your customer" (KYC) checks will have his identity linked to the bitcoins he buys. There are some methods (e.g., buying bitcoins through non-KYC outlets or using coin "mixers") that may allow buyers to achieve some level of privacy, and quite a few developers are working on improving them. But the long-term efficacy of such systems remains to be seen, and it's probably prudent to expect only modest improvements, rather than major ones.

13. Required for Some Important Purpose. 1 out of 5 today but probably 2 out of 5 in the future. Today, there are only a few people/entities that insist on bitcoins as payment. However, as Bitcoin gains prominence, more market participants will likely require it.

14. Backed by a Powerful Agent. 2 out of 5 today, but probably 3 out of 5 in the future. Some black-market participants may seek to defend Bitcoin. Also, nations subject to sanctions may find it useful, possibly even more in the future than today. Some central banks will probably even hold some as reserves someday. The Bank of Japan would be a likely first-mover among developed countries, considering the fact that Japan's government has historically been friendly to Bitcoin and also that holding a noninflationary form of money could offer an interesting way for Japan to solve its crushing debt problem.

Total Score: 47 out of a possible 70 now, but probably 57 out of 70 in the future. Clearly worse overall than dollars today, but slightly better than gold today. Probably significantly better than both dollars and gold in the future!

Figure 9 shows that based on the 14 Characteristics of Good Money, Bitcoin already outscores gold overall and is on its way to outscoring the U.S. dollar. Having recognized this, we can begin to assess Bitcoin as an investment.

Figure 9: Scoring for the 14 Characteristics of Good Money

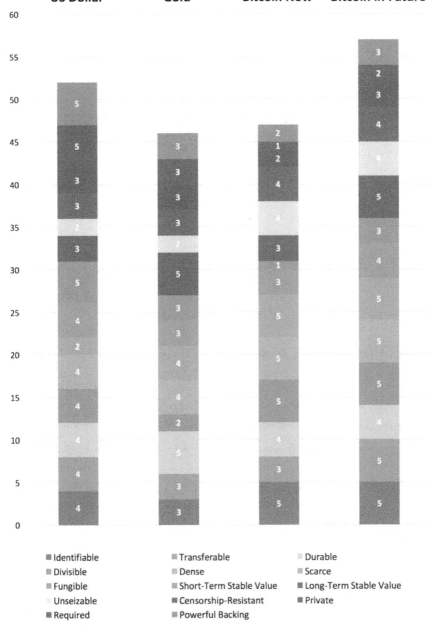

Scoring for the 14 Characteristics of Good Money

US Dollar   Gold   Bitcoin Now   Bitcoin in Future

Legend:
- Identifiable
- Divisible
- Fungible
- Unseizable
- Required
- Transferable
- Dense
- Short-Term Stable Value
- Censorship-Resistant
- Powerful Backing
- Durable
- Scarce
- Long-Term Stable Value
- Private

Chapter 9

The Investment Case for Bitcoin

Bitcoin's strengths don't just rest on how well it scores on the 14 Characteristics of Good Money. In Chapter 6 we examined several other frameworks for analyzing what makes a good money. We will apply these frameworks to Bitcoin, while adding a number of others, all of which will help explain why Bitcoin could be an exceptional investment.

Bitcoin as Growth Asset

As I write this, my son is six years old. Recently I came home after a tough day at work and asked him for a hug. He hopped up and hugged me with all four limbs. I called him a monkey (which I do occasionally). This time he told me, "No, Dad, I'm an ape." He was right. Primates are the larger set (what biologists call an "order") that encompasses great apes, lesser apes, and monkeys. Great apes, lesser apes, and monkeys do not overlap. My wife explained these sets and subsets, and I admitted to my son that I was wrong. Then I told him that he must be a "lesser ape" (owing to his six-year-old stature). "Wrong again, Dad!" My son pointed out that actually he's just a small great ape.

This anecdote illustrates one thing people get wrong about Bitcoin. They look at it and assume it is a more primitive species of money than the dollar and other fiat currencies they deal with on a daily basis. But really Bitcoin is a juvenile specimen of a very advanced species—the most advanced species of money that the world has ever seen. Because it's still a juvenile, it's possible that it will die. But considering the growing community of guardians that has formed around this young monetary system to protect it and foster its development, it seems likely that it will grow all the way to maturity. It already looks both physically strong and technically precocious.

Assessing Bitcoin as a currency today, approximately a decade after its birth, is a bit like looking at Amazon after its first decade. By some accounts, Amazon founder and CEO Jeff Bezos always had the idea that a single website could sell just about anything. But in its early years, the Amazon website was limited to a few areas. At that time, it was a decent bookseller, but it wasn't a great seller of much else. It would take the company years to become an all-purpose retailer. It had to build out its own warehouse and logistics network to reach ever more deeply into U.S. cities, and it also had to expand its data center capacity both to support its own logistics and to sell cloud computing services to third parties.

Bitcoin is the first successful case of an Internet-native solution for money, just as Amazon was the first successful case of an all-purpose Internet retailer. And just as Amazon did, Bitcoin still has to scale up. As Amazon built its data center and warehouse network, Bitcoin is building its network of node operators and miners that provide security to its network. As Amazon matured into a behemoth by the end of its *second* decade of life, Bitcoin has a chance to do the same. A decade into its life, Amazon still had its share of skeptics, and many doubted its ability to grow big enough to justify its valuation. But Amazon's total addressable market was enormous. So, too, is Bitcoin's. Just as Internet-native "growth companies" like Amazon have huge addressable markets, Bitcoin is a "growth currency" with a total addressable market worth tens of trillions of dollars. If Bitcoin takes a significant portion of this market, its value per bitcoin will rise by two orders of magnitude from its current level.

Bitcoin as Uncorrelated Growth Asset

Given that Bitcoin is currently a growth investment asset, we must examine its merit in the context of an overall portfolio. The most popular method is to look at the correlation between its price movement and the price movements of other popular investments. The goal, which is based on the Modern Portfolio Theory of Nobel Prize–winning economist Harry Markowitz[141] and others, is to find assets that have attractive potential rates of return and whose returns are not correlated with other assets in the overall portfolio. Creating a portfolio in this manner reduces the probability that all the assets in the portfolio will lose value at the same time.

For this analysis I will use U.S. stocks (represented by the S&P 500 index), non-U.S. developed market stocks (represented by the MSCI EAFE index), emerging market stocks (represented by the MSCI EM index), bonds (represented by the Barclays Capital US Aggregate Bond Index), and gold. Each of these asset classes represents trillions of dollars in market value, and all are likely to feature prominently in the portfolio of a well-diversified investor. The investment industry standard is to use monthly data, and I will do that here with price data downloaded from Bloomberg. Since Bloomberg's reliable data set for Bitcoin begins on June 30, 2011, I will start there.

Figure 10 is a matrix of the correlations between the returns of these various asset classes. For any two assets, a correlation of 100% means their investment returns move together in lock-stop, a correlation of zero means they move independently with no apparent relation to each other, and a correlation of -100% means they move in opposite directions.

Figure 10: Matrix of Correlations Between Returns on Various Asset Classes

	S&P 500	MSCI EAFE	MSCI Emerging	Barclays Aggregate	Gold	Bitcoin	
S&P 500	100%	84%	71%	-14%	1%	17%	
MSCI EAFE		100%	84%	-4%	12%	14%	Bitcoin
MSCI Emerging			100%	11%	31%	6%	Correlations
Barclays Aggregate				100%	39%	-4%	Less than 20%
Gold					100%	-11%	
Bitcoin						100%	

Data Source: Bloomberg data 6/30/2011–5/31/2019

We can draw a few obvious conclusions from these data. The first is that major stock market asset classes are relatively highly correlated. You do get significant diversification benefit from holding U.S. stocks, foreign developed market stocks, and emerging market stocks over long (multi-year) time periods, but the correlations among these assets are significant based on monthly data.[2] The correlations of S&P/EAFE, S&P/Emerging, and EAFE/Emerging are 84%, 72%, and 84%, respectively. More interesting is the fact that the Barclays Aggregate, gold, and Bitcoin have less than 30% correlation with any of the stock asset classes shown. Bitcoin has less than 15% correlation to *any* of these assets. This is an extraordinary result.

Although the foregoing monthly correlation data present a strong case for Bitcoin as a portfolio diversifier, I don't put too much credence in monthly correlation data. That's because I don't care what happens to my portfolio on a month-to-month basis. Neither should you if you are investing for the long term. One of the key lessons of investing is that some assets are uncorrelated to others *except when you really need them to be.* These "fair-weather" assets are like an insurance policy that doesn't pay when you go to file a claim. Therefore, it's more important to look at an asset's performance in situations where most risk asset classes suffer significant losses, such as in stock bear markets, recessions, and financial crises.

Fortunately for investors, but unfortunately for our analysis, there hasn't been a major global bear market in stocks within Bitcoin's lifetime. The Euro crisis of 2011 was close, as was the more recent trade war scare of late 2018. For the S&P 500 there have been five "corrections" (drops of 10% or more) since the Global Financial Crisis of 2008–2009. We will examine those.

The first S&P 500 correction was April–July 2010, which is arguably too close to the Global Financial Crisis of 2008–2009 to be meaningful, and anyway historical trading prices for Bitcoin aren't available for any dates prior to July 2010 on Bloomberg, Google Finance, or any other reputable source available that I could find.

The second S&P correction (which almost qualified as a bear market) was the Euro crisis of 2011. In this case, the S&P's peak-to-trough drop based on closing prices from April 29, 2011–October 3, 2011 was a 19.4% loss excluding dividends. In the same period, Bitcoin was up 74.3%. Owning bitcoins was very advantageous in this period.

---

2 The diversification benefit of holding different classes of stocks (e.g., emerging markets versus U.S. stocks) has been much greater over longer periods of time. For example, in the first decade of the 21st century, emerging markets stocks performed well while U.S. stocks made zero total return, and in the second decade of the 21st century U.S. stocks have so far dramatically outperformed emerging markets stocks.

The third S&P correction was the Chinese currency devaluation scare in August 2015. In this case, the S&P's drop from July 20, 2015–August 25, 2015 was a 12.2% loss excluding dividends. In the same period, Bitcoin was down 18.6%. Owning bitcoins was disadvantageous.

The fourth S&P correction was the China growth scare of late 2015 and early 2016. In this case, the S&P's drop from November 3, 2015–February 11, 2016 was 13.3% excluding dividends. In the same period, Bitcoin was down only 5.0%. Owning bitcoins was advantageous.

The fifth S&P correction was the trade war and interest rate scare of late 2018. The Trump administration ramped up tariffs against China while the Federal Reserve stated its intent to raise interest rates. In this case, the S&P's drop from October 3, 2018–December 24, 2018 was 19.6% excluding dividends. In the same period, Bitcoin was down 37.0%. Owning bitcoins was disadvantageous.

So in the first measurable case, Bitcoin was up hugely despite stocks being down, in the second it was down quite a bit more than stocks, in the third it was down much less than stocks, and in the fourth and fifth cases it was down quite a bit more than stocks. It's a mixed bag, but Bitcoin provided downside protection versus the S&P 500 in two out of five cases for which we have reliable Bitcoin price data. The bottom line is that in these significant stock market drawdowns, Bitcoin's price appeared to be fairly uncorrelated to the S&P 500 during downturns in the S&P 500.

Bitcoin as Extraordinarily Profitable Uncorrelated Growth Asset

An uncorrelated asset such as Bitcoin is only interesting if it provides attractive investment returns over time. To see how Bitcoin's inclusion in a diversified portfolio affects the overall performance outcome, we will look at a few scenarios. In the first scenario, we assume a portfolio with equal portions of the asset classes above excluding Bitcoin. This results in 20% positions in each of the S&P 500, the MSCI EAFE, the MSCI Emerging Markets, the Barclays Aggregate, and gold. This scenario is illustrated in column 1 of Figure 11. Over the period for which the reliable Bloomberg data for Bitcoin are available and assuming monthly rebalancing of the portfolio to maintain the 20% allocations to each of the five major asset classes, this portfolio produces an annualized return of 4.13% with a standard deviation of 2.65%.

For the second scenario we take 0.2% away from each of the five major asset classes and put that total (0.2% x 5 = 1.0%) into Bitcoin. This is illustrated in column 2 of Figure 11. This portfolio produces an annualized return of 5.75% with a standard deviation of 2.71%. So, adding a 1% position in Bitcoin increases the total return by 1.62% annually, while increasing the standard deviation by just 0.06%.

For the third scenario we get a little more aggressive and take 0.4% away from each of the five major asset classes and put that total 2% into Bitcoin. This is illustrated in column 3 of Figure 11. This portfolio produces an annualized return of 7.35% with a standard deviation of 2.87% (i.e., the portfolio produces 3.22% of annualized return more than the no-Bitcoin portfolio— 7.35% vs. 4.13%), while increasing the standard deviation by less than a quarter of a percentage point. This increase in annualized return of a portfolio makes a huge difference in the long run. The period we have been examining is 7 years and 11 months. (As a reminder, this is not a cherry-picked time interval; it's the full period for which Bloomberg has reliable Bitcoin data.) In this period the no-Bitcoin portfolio grew by a total of 37.8% while the 2% Bitcoin portfolio grew by a total 75.3%. That's the miracle of compound interest. Granted, the investor had to suffer slightly higher portfolio volatility (0.22% additional standard deviation).

Fortunately, it is possible to construct a portfolio that allows us to have our cake (higher returns) and eat it too (lower volatility). For example, let's maintain our 2% Bitcoin position and keep the relative ratios of the non-Bitcoin assets equal to each other but also take two percentage points away from each and put that total 10% into three-month Treasury bills (widely considered to be the global financial market's nearly-risk-free instrument). In this case, the portfolio delivers an annualized return of 7.01% with a standard deviation of 2.63%. This is illustrated in column 4 of Figure 11. Compared with the no-Bitcoin portfolio, this portfolio delivers an annualized return that is 2.88% *higher* and a standard deviation that is 0.02% *lower*. This is the "holy grail" of portfolio management: higher return with lower volatility.

The results of all the foregoing scenarios are listed in the Figure 11 table. What's especially notable about these figures is that they include the most recent period in which Bitcoin is still down over 50% from its peak in December 2017. It's also worth noting that the Bloomberg Bitcoin data, which are the basis for this analysis and subsequent ones, do not include network forks, such as when Bitcoin Cash separated from Bitcoin on August 1, 2017. These events seem to function economically as dividends and therefore raise total returns. If these were included in the analysis, Bitcoin would look even more positive than it does in the figures calculated here.

Figure 11: Portfolio Returns

Scenario Number	1	2	3	4
Scenario Name	No Bitcoin	1% Bitcoin	2% Bitcoin	2% Bitcoin & 10% T-Bills
S&P 500	20.0%	19.8%	19.6%	17.6%
MSCI EAFE	20.0%	19.8%	19.6%	17.6%
MSCI Emerging	20.0%	19.8%	19.6%	17.6%
Barclays Aggregate	20.0%	19.8%	19.6%	17.6%
Gold	20.0%	19.8%	19.6%	17.6%
3-Month Treasury	0.0%	0.0%	0.0%	10.0%
Bitcoin	0.0%	1.0%	2.0%	2.0%
Total	100.0%	100.0%	100.0%	100.0%
Total Return	42.0%	59.3%	78.2%	73.3%
Annualized Return	4.58%	6.12%	7.65%	7.27%
Standard Deviation	2.64%	2.71%	2.88%	2.63%

Bitcoin's Potential Value

Bitcoin's rise in market value from zero at birth over a decade ago to roughly $150 billion as of this writing is remarkable. Yet this valuation is a tiny fraction of its future potential. So now we must ask two questions: (1) How big is the total addressable market, and (2) What share of this market will Bitcoin likely take? I see five major market opportunities for Bitcoin:[142]

1. Digital Gold

Today, the total value of the gold market is roughly $8 trillion. While a portion of this total value arises from industrial (non-monetary) value, as we discussed in Chapter 3, it appears that the majority of the total value of gold is its moneyness (monetary premium). If we assume an industrial value for gold of $2 trillion, then we are left with a monetary value of $6 trillion.

As we saw in Chapter 8, Bitcoin scores significantly higher than gold overall on the 14 Characteristics of Good Money, especially in being more identifiable, transferable, divisible, fungible, censorship-resistant, and unseizable. We should therefore expect Bitcoin to capture a large portion of gold's monetary value over time. A third of this value over the next 10 years seems reasonable. That results in $2 trillion of "gold" value for Bitcoin.

2. Fiat-Beater

As our Chapter 8 scoring demonstrated, Bitcoin is currently on track to becoming better money than the U.S. dollar. Since the dollar is better than any of the world's other fiat currencies, Bitcoin is on its way to becoming better money than the world's fiat currencies in total. Just global coins and bank notes in circulation amount to over $7 trillion. [143] Total money inclusive of demand deposits at banks is over $35 trillion. Total money including time deposits (CDs) exceeds $90 trillion.

In a future in which Bitcoin is prominent, there is likely to be significantly less fractional reserve banking since the market will impose tighter discipline on banks and prevent them from running their balance sheets at 10x leverage. Therefore, the $90 trillion number just mentioned is not relevant. However, some significant fraction of the $7 trillion figure and even the $35 trillion figure is feasible. 20% of $10 trillion seems reasonable, leading to a "fiat" value for Bitcoin of $2 trillion within a decade.

3. Offshore Assets

Nobody knows how much money is held in offshore bank accounts, but reasonable estimates seem to fall into the $10–$30 trillion range.[144] We haven't "scored" offshore assets in this book like we did the dollar, gold, and Bitcoin. However, suffice to say that buying some bitcoins is easier and cheaper than opening a foreign bank account. Today, opening a foreign bank account might still be done anonymously. Buying Bitcoin anonymously today is difficult, but smart software developers are attempting to build anonymity into "second layer" systems atop the Bitcoin network, and some may succeed.

Regardless, for many people holding an offshore asset is not about privacy as much as it's about avoiding unjust seizure. Bitcoin is probably the most unseizable form of money ever created, which means it will surely take some share from the offshore asset market. Assuming conservatively the lower end of the estimated range of offshore assets, $10 trillion, it seems reasonable that Bitcoin could capture 20% of the market within 10 years, leading to an "offshore" value for Bitcoin of $2 trillion.

4. De-Monetizing Other Assets

As we saw in Chapter 2, all goods are at least "a little bit money." However, capital goods in particular are held in part to immunize their owners against the inexorable inflation (value loss) of fiat currencies. Having an inflation-proof asset like Bitcoin reduces the need to hold other "store of value" assets, including real estate or even stocks, partly as hedges against inflation. The classic example is vacant homes in cities, such as London, where long-term empty homes are estimated at over £10 billion ($12 billion).[145]

Once the world wakes up to this fact, some portion of the monetary value of these assets will likely be absorbed by Bitcoin. Global real estate alone is worth more than $200 trillion,[146] and stock markets are worth at least $70 trillion. If the moneyness (monetary premium) embedded in these assets accounts for 10% of their value, and Bitcoin captures a few percentage points, that would lead to a "de-monetization" value of Bitcoin of perhaps $1 trillion.

5. New Applications

As discussed in the prior chapter, ABRA is employing the Bitcoin network to secure a wide range of global assets, as well as facilitate international remittance payments. Microsoft is building a decentralized identity (DID) system to try to solve the problem of identity management and theft on the Internet. The Lightning Network and other scaling solutions could enable micropayments that were impossible with the legacy financial system. There likely will be other applications we haven't even imagined that will rely on Bitcoin, and the development and adoption of these systems will increase demand for Bitcoin. Estimating such incremental demand is impossible, so I will estimate a level of $1 trillion to the "new applications" value of Bitcoin.

Adding up the "gold," "fiat," "offshore," "de-monetization" and "new applications" values of Bitcoin results in a total value of Bitcoin of $8 trillion within the next decade. This is roughly 53x Bitcoin's current value of $150 billion. If these assumptions about the value are reasonable (and I believe they are actually conservative), then we can infer what the market is telling us about the probability of Bitcoin achieving this outcome. It is $150 billion divided by $8 trillion dollars, which equals 1.9%. This isn't quite right since it doesn't factor in the time to realize the potential, but we'll come back to that issue shortly. I believe the probability of achieving this $8 trillion outcome is far higher than 1.9%. I see the probability as greater than 30%.

I approximate my view of the rough "probability distribution" of outcomes for Bitcoin within the next decade as follows: one-third probability that it fails and goes to zero, one-third probability that it becomes a very niche asset and therefore doesn't gain significant value from its current level, and one-third probability of success, approximated as the 53x outcome described earlier. This distribution of possible outcomes makes an investment in Bitcoin (1) as likely to lose value as gain value, yet (2) the most asymmetrically positive investment opportunity I've ever seen. The "expected value" of this bet is 1/3 x 0 + 1/3 x 1 + 1/3 * 53 = 18x my investment over 10 years. That's an expected annualized return of 33%, or approximate doubling of value every 2.5 years.

I don't expect to see another investment opportunity as attractive as this ever again in my lifetime. How could it go wrong? Lots of ways. Let's examine them in the following chapters.

Chapter 10

Technical Risks to Bitcoin

So what could go wrong on Bitcoin's path to world domination? Plenty. Not all juveniles reach adulthood. The next few chapters should not be considered an exhaustive list of things that could harm or kill Bitcoin. However, they do catalogue what I see as the most significant of the risks that could conceivably prevent Bitcoin from reaching its potential. In aggregate, I believe these risks have perhaps a one-third probability of taking down Bitcoin within the next decade. If Bitcoin doesn't fail, its value has a good chance of moving much higher.

In the remaining chapters of this book we will examine these risks. They have been grouped into four categories of risk: (1) technical, (2) political, (3), economic, and (4) sociological and psychological. These groupings are somewhat arbitrary, and a number of the risks touch more than one of these categories. In such cases, I have attempted to categorize each risk based on its primary risk category.

This chapter addresses the technical risks.

Obsolescence Risk and Competitive Moat

No technology is immune to obsolescence. Some people argue that Bitcoin is just the "first of its kind" and will be replaced by a better version, just as Facebook replaced MySpace, Google replaced Yahoo!, and Microsoft

Explorer replaced Netscape Navigator. This argument is based on a misunderstanding of the history of digital money. Bitcoin is not the first digital currency. It was preceded by published designs such as Bit Gold and B-money that weren't implemented and by actually-implemented digital currencies such as DigiCash and E-gold that ultimately failed.[147,148] Bitcoin is therefore already the successful technology that replaced prior failed ones.

Moreover, the examples of Internet-based applications such as social networks, search algorithms, and Internet browsers cited in the prior paragraph don't require nearly the level of trust that a form of money does. Bitcoin's competitive "moat" against potential usurpers includes its brand, its existing status as reserve currency among existing cryptocurrencies, its robust security model, and its vibrant community of supporters. But most important is its experience of battle-testing as a multi-billion-dollar target for hackers and other attackers. Only the experience of attacks over time can build the track record of success that a new form of money requires. If Bitcoin reaches maturity and becomes widely adopted as a medium of exchange, its network effect and leadership position will be very difficult to displace.

Reliance on the Internet

Bitcoin depends on the Internet. Its ongoing functioning requires communication across a distributed network of computers that can share data via telecom networks. The destruction of the Internet might spell doom for Bitcoin. In the early days of the Internet, its destruction might have been possible. Quite a few Luddites sounded alarms regarding the Internet's enabling of crime and social ills. Today the world is still grappling with these issues and others, including destruction of privacy and monetization of personal data by giant Internet monopolists. As mentioned earlier, some of these latter issues may even be solvable using some of the encryption and decentralization principles underlying Bitcoin. Regardless, even in the presence of these downsides of the Internet, society's dependence on Internet-based services make it extraordinarily unlikely that the Internet will be shut down by any government entity or be destroyed by anything else.

It's worth considering that if the Internet fails permanently or for a long period of time, many other risk assets will also be vulnerable. Say goodbye to trillions of dollars' worth of Internet companies, payment systems, free information, etc. Moreover, since so much of the world's computing activity has moved to the "cloud" (which depends on Internet connectivity), and since computing permeates most areas of life, loss of the Internet would have huge commercial and even health-related consequences. So worrying about Internet failures bringing down Bitcoin is a little like worrying about whether the detonation of a nuclear bomb 10 miles from your house is going to adversely affect the stock market. You might have bigger problems to worry about!

One possible future scenario, proposed by former Google Chairman Eric Schmidt, would be a bifurcation of the Internet between China and the West.[149] If China were to manage to completely block Internet access to the outside world, a feat it has not achieved up to this point, the result could be a split between "China Bitcoin" and "Non-China Bitcoin." This outcome seems unlikely given that Bitcoin's bandwidth requirements are so low that small cracks in the "Great Firewall," whether in the form of satellite Internet links, point-to-point radio-based data transmission, or other means, would likely allow Chinese users access to the Bitcoin network despite the government's best efforts.

Hacking of the Bitcoin Ledger by Breaking the Encryption

Many people still talk about Bitcoin getting hacked. This is a major misunderstanding. The distributed architecture and the cryptographic hashing system make the Bitcoin ledger extraordinarily secure. Indeed, the system's resilience to hacking is one of its major selling points. The Bitcoin ledger itself appears never to have been hacked. The hacks and consumer losses that people talk about are actually due to mishandling of private keys. The private key (password) is what provides secure access to your bitcoins. Fundamentally, bitcoins are bearer assets, so if you lose the key, you lose the asset.

Fortunately, you can handle Bitcoin securely if you know what you're doing. Moreover, there are numerous companies and organizations currently developing better systems for management of private keys. This means that in the future people will have access to a menu of options for securing their bitcoins that range from self-managed deep cold storage to hybrid solutions involving trusted third parties.

Related to the perceived risk of a hack of the blockchain is the risk of a "back door" weakness purposefully written into the software. This is extraordinarily unlikely because Bitcoin has already existed for a decade as open-source software "in the wild." Anyone in the world who has Internet access can audit the code, and probably tens of thousands of people have done so. This intense level of scrutiny makes hiding malicious code nearly impossible, especially since the Bitcoin software is so simple compared to many modern software programs. Bitcoin's software started with just a few thousand lines of codes, and the most common Bitcoin Core implementation is still only around a hundred thousand lines.[150] For comparison, Microsoft Windows has tens of millions of lines.[151]

Prior to launching the network, Bitcoin's creator(s) would have known that mining and maintaining the operation of the network in its infancy would likely fall primarily to him/her/them, which would result in the accumulation of a significant number of bitcoins. It is believed that the founder(s) of Bitcoin owns a significant number of bitcoins, worth billions of dollars at current prices as a result of mining in the early years when the rate of issuance of new bitcoins was higher. It seems very unlikely that Bitcoin's creator would risk destroying a multi-billion-dollar fortune by destroying confidence in Bitcoin. He/she/they would have realized that creating a durable and secure network would be far more profitable than creating one with a security hole and attempting to "exit scam" the system—even if the founder(s) thought he/she/they could sneak it past the thousands of programmers crawling all over the open-source code. This logic assumes that the founder(s) is/are even still alive today. There is a contingent within the Bitcoin community that believes the founder(s) died years ago, and it is possible that the founder(s)' bitcoins are lost forever along with the private keys that control them.

The cryptographic tools used in Bitcoin (primarily SHA-256 and ECDSA described in Chapter 7) have been used and field-tested for decades. They are therefore believed to be secure. However, they have not been *mathematically proven* to be unsolvable (other than by brute force computation). It's therefore theoretically possible that they could be broken by new mathematical solutions or computational techniques not yet invented.

Quantum computers, which have recently made it off the drawing board and into the laboratory in recent years, could eventually become capable of breaking Bitcoin's encryption, especially ECDSA. But thus far the history of cryptography has demonstrated that the encoders have been able to stay ahead of the codebreakers by developing better encryption techniques. It seems likely this will continue to be true since "quantum-resistant" encryption techniques are currently under development to meet the challenge of the quantum computers. However, if the Bitcoin network were to implement a stronger form of encryption in response to a new technique (quantum computing or otherwise) for breaking Bitcoin's security, such an implementation might require the network to "hard fork" to a new version. This would require the network node operators to upgrade to the new version, and such an event could be disruptive.

Hardware Back Doors

Another potential "back door" into the Bitcoin network could be via the mining hardware. It is theoretically possible that Bitmain or one of the other large manufacturers of Bitcoin mining hardware could have included circuitry in its ASICs that allows someone to effectively flip a switch and take over the hardware remotely via an Internet connection.

This sort of risk appears quite unlikely due to scanning technology that allows scrutiny of the circuitry of the ASICs used to mine Bitcoin. Bitcoin ASICs are much simpler than motherboards for personal computers and commonly used data center servers. ASICs are designed solely to perform the SHA-256 hash calculation, which is far less complex than the functions that most computers perform. If anyone were to examine mining equipment and discover a back door, the manufacturer's future equipment sales would likely go to zero instantly. Nobody wants to buy mining equipment that can be instantly deactivated by the manufacturer! Since the Bitcoin ASIC manufacturing business is probably worth billions of dollars as of this writing, it appears extremely unlikely that the major hardware manufacturers would risk their profits by including back doors in their products.

Notwithstanding that it is already low, this hardware back door risk will probably reduce further over time as the ASIC manufacturing business becomes larger (and therefore more equity value is at stake). The risk will also probably reduce as the rate of improvement in ASIC circuitry slows. The industry has already reached seven-nanometer spacing on its chips,[152] which is approaching the maximum transistor density possible before quantum effects lead to interference. Such effects limit further miniaturization based on existing two-dimensional silicon-based chip architecture. Three-dimensional (stacked) chip architecture will probably emerge eventually, but that could take years.

Centralization

As discussed earlier, Bitcoin's high (and rising) scores on the 14 Characteristics of Good Money are most pronounced in the key attributes of being (1) scarce, (2) unseizable, and (3) censorship-resistant. These characteristics depend on Bitcoin's immutability, which depends on Bitcoin's decentralization. Such decentralization is relevant to each of the major sets of participants in the network, including (1) miners and mining pools, (2) mining equipment manufacturers, (3) non-mining node operators, (4) owners of bitcoins, (5) software developers, (6) exchanges and businesses, and (7) Internet service providers. If any one of these groups becomes too centralized, it could potentially threaten the network. Let's examine each in turn.

1. Miners and Mining Pools
In Bitcoin's early days, there were very few computers supporting the network. But as it grew, the total mining capacity (hashpower) also grew dramatically. As mentioned earlier, this meant that miners had to band together into pools in order to have any hope of getting paid via a block subsidy (newly minted bitcoins and transaction fees) with any frequency. Today, it appears that the largest pool has roughly 20% share of the total network's mining capacity, and several other pools have at least 10%.[153] Although individual mining operators have the freedom to leave the pool they mine with, the pool operators have some ability to manipulate the system, especially since most of them have the ability to select which transactions get included in the blocks their members are mining. There are currently proposals in the works, such as "Betterhash", that could shift some of the power away from these pools.[154]

2. Mining Equipment Manufacturers

In the last few years, a single manufacturer, Bitmain, has produced the majority of Bitcoin mining equipment, some of which it has sold to other mining operations, and some of which it has kept for its own mining use. Fortunately, there are signs that other equipment manufacturers are increasingly able to compete with Bitmain.

3. Non-Mining Node Operators

Much more numerous than the miners are the non-mining node operators. These don't participate in the proof of work system, but they do validate transactions.[155] Numbering in the thousands globally, it is these node operators that validate and propagate transactions across the network globally. They serve as a check on the power of the miners because they can reject blocks of transactions that do not conform to the consensus rules specified in the Bitcoin code.

4. Owners of Bitcoins

Owners of large blocks of bitcoins can manipulate markets and perhaps bribe miners or node operators in extreme cases. In the long run, if the ownership of bitcoins is too concentrated, it's possible that the system will be deemed a concentrated plutocracy that average users therefore deem illegitimate.

5. Software Developers

The software developers are extraordinarily important to the Bitcoin network because software upgrades and bug fixes don't happen automatically. Historically the "Bitcoin Core" development team has comprised a few key developers and scores of other significant contributors. An informal system governs the process by which upgrades get "merged" into the core software. All parties have an important check against the software developers by virtue of the software's open-source nature, which allows anyone to scrutinize it and catch errors or unscrupulous changes. Furthermore, no miner or node operator is forced to adopt new versions of the software. A miner or node operator can operate a version of the software that is several years old because the newer/improved versions are "backwards compatible" with the older versions. Such backwards-compatibility makes the overall network more robust since it allows node operators to take their time upgrading to improved versions of Bitcoin.

6. Exchanges and Businesses

Exchanges that allow trading from dollars and other currencies into Bitcoin and vice versa can be a centralizing force, especially to the extent that people leave their bitcoins "on deposit" at the exchanges. Also, other businesses that are influential in the Bitcoin economy have in the past attempted to exert influence on the system. Fortunately, history indicates that no exchange or business or group thereof has actually succeeded in attempts to exert any significant amount of control over Bitcoin.

7. Internet Service Providers

Arguably anything that allows the Internet to function is also important to the Bitcoin network. But perhaps the only significant *physical* chokepoints are the Internet service providers (ISPs). In most countries there are a few companies that run the Internet's infrastructure, and they collocate in key interconnection points, such as 60 Hudson Street in New York. The ISP companies and their physical network equipment are at risk of consolidation and control. Fortunately, the Internet, and specifically its TCP/IP protocol, was designed to route traffic around chokepoints. This means that even if a majority of routes get co-opted, Internet data packet traffic (including communication across the Bitcoin network) should still be able to propagate effectively.

Mining Attacks on the Bitcoin Network

As discussed in Chapter 7, miners attempt to solve the proof of work, and if they do, they collect the block subsidy of newly minted bitcoins and also the transaction fees attached to each transaction submitted by the network's users. However, a malicious miner can "attack" the network in several ways. While this list is not exhaustive, there are arguably three primary classes of attacks that a miner could perpetrate against the network: (1) refuse to validate legitimate transactions (i.e., block them and thereby mine empty or partially empty transaction blocks), (2) double-spend bitcoins in addresses for which he has the private keys, or (3) if he can muster a majority of the mining power of the entire network, reverse transactions in recent history. Let's examine each of these scenarios.

The case of mining empty blocks has a similar effect as a "denial of service" (DoS) attack on a website. In a DoS attack, the attacker attempts to deny legitimate users access to the website by overwhelming the website's servers with requests to access the webpage. In the case of Bitcoin, the attacker mines empty blocks, which amounts to solving the proof of work problem without including any transaction requests. This conforms with the network consensus rules while effectively censoring transactions on the network. This has the effect of the network being down (so users can't send transactions) in the time periods in which the empty blocks are mined. The outcome is analogous to your online bank account being inaccessible when a hacker is DoS-attacking your bank's servers. You'd like to send money, but you don't have access to the system while it's under attack. Once the attack ends, you regain access.

In contrast, double-spending bitcoins means that the attacker sends bitcoins to someone in exchange for something else (asset/good/service), and then re-mines the transaction block to undo the payment such that he gets his bitcoins back and keeps the asset/good/service he just paid for. Lastly, if the attacker manages to muster a majority of the total mining power of the Bitcoin network in a "51% attack," he can, over time, re-mine transaction blocks back into history and reverse transactions from the recent past.

It's important to note that none of these outcomes allows the attacker to disrupt bitcoins in addresses that have not been transferred during the period for which the attacker is mining or re-mining transaction blocks. Moreover, none of these outcomes allows the attacker to steal any bitcoins from addresses for which he doesn't have the private key. The only way the attacker can "steal" bitcoins is via the double-spend scenario described earlier. This point is poorly understood by people who assume that an attack on the system results in the entire structure falling apart. The reality is much less dire.

If the attacker manages to attack the network continuously and painstakingly re-solve the proofs-of-work for recent blocks, then what he *can* do is reverse transactions that occurred in the recent past. If you sent bitcoins in one of those recent blocks, then your transaction could be reversed, and since an attacker can undo recent transactions, that does mean that if someone sent *you* bitcoins in a recent transaction, you may lose those bitcoins. They don't move into the attacker's account; they simply return to the sender. So the attacker can wreak a certain amount of havoc on your account, but at no profit to himself, unless you gave him something valuable in exchange for bitcoins, and he reversed that transaction (the double-spend scenario described earlier).

This is why the standard for deeming a transaction as "finalized" is to wait for six 10-minute blocks (one hour) to transpire. Provided that the attacker does not have control of a majority of the entire mining power of the network, it becomes exponentially harder to reorganize the blockchain with the addition of each incremental block. So there's actually no such thing as true finality—only a vanishingly small and continuously shrinking chance of a transaction being reversed. While this may sound scary, we must remember that transactions in the banking system get reversed frequently. There is no such thing as a "done deal" in any monetary system. Having said this, and acknowledged that nothing is irreversible, I still contend that, for all the reasons just discussed, Bitcoin is in fact the most immutable monetary ledger in existence or likely to be in existence for the foreseeable future.

All of these kinds of mining attacks are expensive to execute. In the case of mining empty transaction blocks, the attacker has to use a lot of costly electricity to run the mining equipment to perpetrate the attack, but he doesn't collect any transaction fees. In the case of a double-spending attack or a 51% attack, success means damaging confidence in the Bitcoin network, which impairs the value of the block subsidy and transaction fees collected by miners. Since the value of the expensive mining equipment is based on the block subsidies and transaction fees it can generate over time, attacking the network impairs the value of the mining equipment used to perpetrate the attack. So the attacker has strong financial incentives *not* to perpetrate such an attack. Additionally, depending on the resources of the attacker, the attack may only be successful part of the time, unless the attacker can somehow muster a majority of the entire network's mining capacity.

Coordinating a majority of the network's mining capacity without coercion via threat of violence would be extraordinarily expensive. It would require buying or renting a majority of the world's existing ASIC capacity. Acquiring such a large portion of this capacity would be akin to attempting to corner the market for a resource. Mining operators and equipment manufacturers would likely get wind of the enormous demand and charge higher prices for their equipment.

One way of mitigating the cost of such an attack could be by taking a "short" position in Bitcoin (i.e., betting against the price of bitcoins). This could be accomplished in one of several ways: by opening a "cash" short position with some market counterparty (such as a Bitcoin exchange), by taking a short position in the Bitcoin futures market, or by buying put options in the Bitcoin options market. The concept of shorting an asset and then attacking it is not unique to Bitcoin. Countless financial assets worldwide, including stocks, can be shorted by attackers who stand to profit from causing damage to the asset.

For example, an unscrupulous attacker could short the stock of an oil company before sabotaging a well or a tanker. However, putting on a short position large enough to make a difference in the cost of a Bitcoin attack would require finding multiple counterparties willing to take the opposite side of the trade *and* also being able to collect from them once they realized an attack was in progress and they'd been manipulated by the attacker. Both opening the positions and closing them profitably would probably be quite difficult. Short-selling counterparties generally aren't stupid. They recognize the possibility of an attacker trying to fleece them and are therefore likely to be vigilant about both (1) the overall size of the short market, and (2) signs of collusion among short sellers that might tip them off to an impending attack.

Double-spend attacks have already been witnessed on cryptocurrencies such as Ethereum Classic[156] and Verge[157] that are orders of magnitude weaker than Bitcoin. In particular, these two cryptocurrencies had "hash rates" (total computational power on their networks dedicated to mining and therefore network security) that were orders of magnitude lower than Bitcoin's. They were also mineable with general purpose graphics processing units (GPUs). Such equipment can be easily repurposed between different weaker cryptocurrencies, which means that an attacker can easily rent GPU mining capacity from other cryptocurrency networks in order to mount an attack. The attacks took the form of sending the cryptocurrency to an exchange, swapping it for Bitcoin, and then attempting to re-write the Bitcoin ledger and thereby achieve a double-spend. Interestingly, although these attacks were initially successful, they ultimately failed because the exchanges withheld the proceeds of the double-spends. Somewhat surprisingly, these cryptocurrencies proved resilient even after the attacks. Their prices were almost unaffected.

In contrast to the weaknesses in these cryptocurrencies that were attacked, Bitcoin has evolved to require ASICs, which greatly increase the network's security, as discussed in Chapter 7. Considering the ingenuity of Bitcoin's economic incentive structure and the fact that Bitcoin's mining network is now fully based on specialized ASICs, it appears that a successful mining attack would have to be done for noneconomic reasons, such as in the case of a government seeking to damage or destroy Bitcoin. We will consider this risk in the next chapter.

Chapter 11

Political Risks to Bitcoin

Political risks are another major category of risks facing Bitcoin. This chapter will address the risks that are primarily political in nature.

Government Attacks

Eventually there may be a western government crackdown on cryptocurrencies. From the perspective of governments, there are several major problems with cryptocurrencies: (1) potential facilitation of criminal commerce (providing payment systems for trafficking contraband or funding terrorism), (2) loss of seigniorage profit from printing money, and (3) general loss of control, including power of confiscation.

Governments could already do a lot more to deter crime by placing certain restrictions on regular fiat currencies rather than by attempting to control Bitcoin. A study by Ruth Judson of the Federal Reserve in 2012 estimated that three quarters of all hundred-dollar bills were located outside the United States.[158] As of December 2017 the Federal Reserve reported that hundred-dollar bills accounted for $1.252 trillion of the total $1.571 trillion dollars of currency in circulation globally, or 80% of the total.[159] In its latest figures (January 31, 2019), the Federal Reserve reported total currency in circulation of $1.7 trillion.[160] Assuming the same 80% ratio, that would imply $1.354 trillion of hundred-dollar bills in circulation. Using Judson's estimate that three quarters of hundred-dollar bills circulate outside the United States implies *over $1 trillion of hundred-dollar bills circulating in foreign countries.*

Hundred-dollar bills aren't too useful for buying bread and milk, especially in poorer countries where a single such bill represents a week's wages! Granted, a significant portion of these C-notes are used legitimately as stores of value. But a significant portion are undoubtedly used for criminal activities. So if you object to Bitcoin on the grounds that criminals use it, or think that government should outlaw it for that reason, you may be barking up the wrong tree. Dollars are the preferred criminal money. (We'll delve more into this topic in a later section).

Some prominent economists, such as Ken Rogoff at Harvard, have argued that we should do away with high-denomination bills or even all cash entirely, which would allow governments to monitor every financial transaction that occurs between their citizens.[161] I don't believe that a free society can exist without the ability to transact privately. Nevertheless, even if the U.S. government or a coalition of western democracies unite in an effort to restrict cryptocurrencies (a big "if" considering they haven't been able to link arms on many other issues), geopolitics suggests they won't be able to cooperate with countries like China and Russia or other non-western or developing countries. Therefore, Bitcoin will survive in some major markets even if it doesn't in the United States.

Furthermore, a large portion of the Bitcoin miners are located in China. That makes it less likely that China would completely ban Bitcoin. In 2017 Chinese authorities did halt the activities of cryptocurrency exchanges in the country, but it seems that trading continues among over-the-counter dealers and in peer-to-peer formats. Since Bitcoin has already provided a capital escape valve for many Chinese, there may be an ongoing struggle between Communist Party officials who want to ban it to contain capital flight, and officials and wealthy Chinese citizens who already own it and want to see its value rise!

China has another interest in seeing Bitcoin succeed. For the better part of a century, the United States has enjoyed the "exorbitant privilege" of printing the world's reserve currency. While China might prefer that the yuan become the world's dominant currency, it seems reasonable that China will settle for a multi-currency world in which Bitcoin plays a significant role and China has a major role in supporting and profiting from the Bitcoin network. On April 8, 2019, Reuters reported that China's state planning agency, the National Development and Reform Commission (NRDC), was considering eliminating Bitcoin mining in the country and seeking public comment on the idea.[162] Although China removing its mining capacity would remove one of the major risks to the Bitcoin network and therefore be positive for a Bitcoin investment, I suspect China won't ban Bitcoin. More likely, the Chinese government is flexing its muscles in an attempt to gain more control over it. Time will tell.

The attraction of Bitcoin may be substantially larger in poor or corrupt countries than in the United States. Imagine you are an entrepreneur in Nigeria or Russia who is at risk of having your bank accounts seized by the government for political or other purposes. You might prefer to deal in bitcoins rather than in naira or rubles. Or imagine you are a businessperson in India. You want to sign a long-term contract with a supplier, but you know that if the deal sours and you have to sue him to recover your money, the case will take a decade to crawl through India's court system. Maybe you instead make a deal based on a "smart contract" escrow system on the Bitcoin network and dispense with the usual legal enforcement mechanisms. You may be especially keen on avoiding the rupia considering the 2016 fiasco discussed in Chapter 8 in which the Indian government eliminated all the high-denomination bills in a botched effort to crack down on tax evasion. Who needs that kind of risk with their money?

Key to a potential government attack is timing. Legislative action would require concerted effort by the United States as well as European governments. There is little evidence that legislators are interested in destroying Bitcoin, and the reasons for this are clear. The genie is already out of the bottle and putting it back in is probably impossible. Millions of Americans already own Bitcoin, and outlawing ownership of this asset would amount to a significant destruction of property given that the total market value of Bitcoin is roughly $150 billion, and the broader cryptocurrency market is almost double that size.

The history of prohibition in the United States and other countries is ugly. The major lesson has been that goods that people want to use and that are hard to confiscate will continue to be widely used even when they are prohibited by government. Moreover, prohibition on such goods pushes business into the hands of criminals, which causes the spread of organized crime and violence, as in the cases of alcohol prohibition in the 1920s and the "drug war" that is still ongoing today.

In the United States the only significant precedent for a *monetary* seizure/prohibition was Executive Order 6102 signed by President Franklin Delano Roosevelt on April 5, 1933, which forbade "hoarding" of gold or silver coins or bullion or currency.[163] This policy was actionable only in the context of the worst economic calamity of the twentieth century, the Great Depression. It could not be maintained absent such extraordinary circumstances, and it was eventually reversed.

Notwithstanding the obstacles to government intervention, it's still worth asking what would happen if all the world's major governments were to overcome their inability to coordinate globally and did decide to blacklist Bitcoin. It would still be very difficult to kill Bitcoin because Bitcoin is like a weed that is nearly impossible to eradicate. One instructive precedent is BitTorrent, the world's most popular peer-to-peer file-sharing service. It exists primarily for users to share illegally pirated video content. Copyright law is one of the more zealously enforced areas of law. As a result, BitTorrent has been attacked and pursued by governments all over the world for years. Yet experts believe that it still accounts for more than 4% of worldwide Internet traffic![164] BitTorrent is so hard to destroy because (1) people like to use it, and (2) it's decentralized. Bitcoin is the same. Distributed Internet-native peer-to-peer systems like these are extraordinarily resilient.

Government Control versus the Innovation Imperative

Another key reason governments haven't attempted to outlaw Bitcoin or other cryptocurrencies is the need to foster innovation. As discussed in Chapter 7, Bitcoin has already made a strong claim to being "The Internet of Money." Bitcoin's potential as a global money is our focus here, but the story of cryptocurrencies is much bigger, and part of what makes it bigger is the extraordinary innovations it has fostered. That story is beyond the scope of this book, and much of it is summarized in Alex and Don Tapscott's *Blockchain Revolution: How the Technology Behind Bitcoin Is Changing Money, Business, and the World*, published in 2016.

However, more recently the need for blockchain-based and cryptocurrency-based innovation has been clarified and made more urgent because of the way the giants of the Internet, especially Google, Facebook, Amazon and Microsoft, have wielded increasingly monopolistic power in the marketplace. They have the potential to do harm to our society, and have already realized much of that potential, while innovations spurred by the cryptocurrency-based systems have the potential to counter a lot of the effects of their monopolistic behavior.

On May 15, 2016, I wrote a Letter to the Editor of *The Economist* highlighting the monopoly behavior of the Internet giants (e.g., Google, Facebook, Amazon, Microsoft). When the magazine published it in the next issue, I was flattered. But when I saw that the cover article of the following issue was about the monopolistic behavior of these companies, I knew I was really on to something. Two years later, in 2018, I found myself explaining the perniciousness of these monopoly effects to my clients by returning to some of the most basic concepts in economics.

Here's how the Internet monopolist behavior works. We'll start with the basics. Imagine you are hungry for lunch and you go to the corner deli. You see that a turkey sandwich is $10. You love turkey sandwiches, and you would happily pay as much as $14 for a decent turkey sandwich. If you can buy it for $10, that's a great trade because you are paying $10 for something that is worth $14 to you. The $4 difference is what the economists call "consumer surplus." Now suppose that the sandwich shop has figured out that it can make the turkey sandwich at a total cost of $8. If it can sell the sandwich for $10, then it captures $2 of what economists call "producer surplus" but the rest of us just call "profit." (Economists are not immune to the temptation to give more complicated names to things that already have simple names, and Bitcoin enthusiasts are guilty of the same.)

Now let's add in the monopoly behavior. Suppose that the company operating the deli leases all the best deli locations in your town and manages to squeeze out competitors. It used to be that if a deli raised the price of its turkey sandwich above $10, it would lose business to the deli down the street that was willing to charge only $10. But now with that competitor gone, the deli monopolist can set the price of a turkey sandwich at $12. The deli has managed to capture an additional $2 of surplus from you. You're still willing to buy the sandwich, since it's worth $14 to you, but your consumer surplus of $4 has fallen to $2, and that $2 difference went straight into the pocket of the monopolist. Good news for the monopolist; bad news for you.

The advertising-based Internet monopolists, such as Facebook and Google, have taken it a step further. With these companies, when you go to the register to pay for your "sandwich"—in this case you're instead buying "social network" or "search" services—and you ask what it costs, they say, "Sorry, we don't accept dollars; instead you have to give us your personal behavioral data." You reasonably ask, "Oh, ok, what are my data worth?" They reply, "Don't worry about it."

Think about this transaction. In order to buy the product, *you are trading away something you don't know the value of.* Your grandmother could tell you there's a word for this kind of a transaction. It's called a "swindle." History is full of swindlers who try to get people to part with something they don't know the value of in a transaction that benefits the swindler. Facebook and Google have taken this activity to a scale never before witnessed in the history of private enterprise.

In March 2019 Harvard psychologist Shoshana Zuboff published *Surveillance Capitalism,* which seems likely to be the definitive text on the underlying problems with the Internet monopolists. Facebook, for example, has not only led the way in the ongoing personal data swindle that these companies perpetrate, but has also failed to protect its users' privacy, and could possibly have helped swing the most recent United States presidential election under dubious circumstances. It has done this while disavowing any responsibility for the content on its platform or the "echo chamber" effects of its habit of feeding its users only the information and opinions they want to hear. Facebook now appears to be slightly modifying its corporate strategy in response to the public outcry over these issues.[165] Meanwhile, Google, which share's some of Facebooks problems due to its similar advertising-based business model, spends more on direct lobbying ($17 million in 2018) than any other company in America.[166]

It seems we might finally be reaching a turning point at which a substantial portion of the public comes to realize that these companies (1) swindle us by giving us near-zero-marginal-cost-to-produce services that are worth far less than the data we feed them, (2) destroy our privacy by hoovering up our data and selling it to third parties,[167] (3) effectively hack the primitive portion of our brains by providing serotonin hits for "likes" and interactions that are addictive in nature and make us unhappier overall,[168] (4) reduce our ability to concentrate and reason due to such constant stimulation,[169] (5) create polarizing and hatred-cultivating echo chambers,[170] (6) spread misinformation that can result in the weakening of democracy,[171] (7) turn journalism into a click-bait-driven business model, and (8) possibly even destroy jobs and livelihoods by accelerating the rate of automation in the American economy.[172]

At the time of this writing, I personally hold shares of Google and Facebook, and my clients also have ownership stakes in these stocks, primarily through exchange-traded funds and mutual funds. So I want these companies to perform well. I also hope they change their business models to mitigate the harm they do. However, the existence of shareholders like me and my clients makes that unlikely. Corporations' primary fiduciary duty is to maximize profits for their investors, and the existing business models are extraordinarily profitable.

More likely is a regulatory push to limit these companies' abuses. Monopolists have always been subject to regulation for economic reasons that are mostly noncontroversial. Unfortunately, regulation is double-edged even with respect to consumer protection because regulations create compliance costs that the largest monopolists are able to afford more easily than smaller upstart competitors. This perversely widens the competitive moat the monopolists enjoy. We have seen this dynamic play out not only in banking (as covered in Chapter 3), but in telecom, cable TV, pharmaceuticals, and various other industries.

At this point, it's not clear how aggressive the move to regulate these companies will be. Microsoft, Google, Facebook, and Amazon are all based in the United States. American politicians and regulators know that if they had over-regulated the Internet in its nascency, some of these companies might instead have been built in Europe, India, China, or Russia, and policy makers may rightly still fear what would happen if they were to go after any of these companies now. European countries have levied fines in the billions on these companies; here in the U.S. the fines have been in the millions, a barely noticeable slap on the wrist. That may be changing, but even fines in the billions matter little given the size of these companies. They are effectively just a "cost of doing business."

The good news is that cryptocurrency-based systems hold the possibility of allowing software developers to build social networks and other Internet-native tools that allow their individual users to at least (1) decide how much of their personal information they choose to share, (2) capture more of the surplus generated by selling this information to advertisers who monetize their attention, (3) customize and limit the amount of advertiser manipulation they suffer, and (4) customize their news feeds to be more objective.

There are already thousands of brilliant software developers and entrepreneurs working on these systems in a movement known as "Internet 3.0" or "Web 3.0." These people aren't all altruists looking to put money back into the pockets of users. They also have self-interested motivations, because consumers aren't the only ones who are being exploited by the existing surveillance capitalist system. Software developers and other entrepreneurs are also among the monopolists' victims. This is because in the last decade and a half the Internet behemoths became "platforms" upon which additional software applications were built, such as games on Facebook and recruiting tools on LinkedIn. The entrepreneurs and software developers who created these valuable applications have already learned the hard way that they are giving a free call option on their businesses to the Internet monopolists. If an application/business fails, no harm is done to the monopolist platform company. But if it succeeds, the platform monopolist can just kick the successful application off the platform, build out the same functionality, and capture the value!

Apple, Google, Amazon, and Microsoft are the most valuable companies in the world today and they are all based on the Internet. Now, cryptocurrencies based on the same technology as Bitcoin offer the possibility of creating Internet-native networks that put more of the producer surplus captured by these companies back into the pockets of ordinary voters, all while supporting the broader technology ecosystems of software developers and other talented and high-earning taxpayers in the United States. Just as aggressive regulation of the Internet giants might have led them to flee the United States, attempts to prohibit or excessively regulate Bitcoin or other cryptocurrency projects will send these people to greener pastures and hand the benefits of the next major generation of Internet-based economies to foreign countries. Despite its shortcomings, the United States government is unlikely to make such a catastrophic mistake. People in government know that innovation is what propels America's economic and military success, and they are probably wise enough not to kill the golden goose.

It's not impossible that certain factions in government (such as those politicians who have been captured by the Internet giants and now seek to protect them from competition) could make the major mistake of trying to quash the innovations stemming from the cryptocurrency developers. However, the level of partisan gridlock in the legislatures of the U.S. and other democratic countries casts doubt on their abilities to reach consensus on legislation to impede Bitcoin and other cryptocurrencies. Furthermore, once a substantial percentage of citizens own the asset, they are going to fight to prevent any actions that damage the value of their investment. This dynamic became evident in South Korea in 2017 when the government attempted to crack down on Bitcoin and other cryptocurrencies. The reaction was dramatic. Hundreds of thousands of Koreans signed petitions to prevent the government from crushing their "happy dream" of cryptocurrencies.[173] Once a certain percentage of Americans owns Bitcoin or other cryptocurrencies, they will vote to protect their investments.

Terrorism and Criminality

One event that might spur Congress and the President to action would be clear evidence that a terrorist group or specific attack was funded with Bitcoin. A terrorist attack on U.S. soil that is directly linked to payments of bitcoins could deal a severe blow to Bitcoin's future. At that point, the debate would be between the anti-terrorist hawks and the libertarians who don't want the government excessively regulating nascent industries.

Fortunately, the risk of a terrorist attack being funded with bitcoins, and the risk of criminal activity using the Bitcoin network, are dramatically reduced by the auditability of the Bitcoin blockchain. The news media love to publish fearmongering clickbait headlines on the use of Bitcoin by criminals, but this is one of the most inaccurate characterizations of Bitcoin prevalent today. On August 7, 2018, Bloomberg reported that according to a member of the DEA (Drug Enforcement Agency) 10-person Cyber Investigative Task Force, which coordinates with the FBI and the ATF, the use of cryptocurrencies in criminal activity had shrunk from about 90% of transactions in 2013 to 10% in 2018.[174] Subsequently, former DEA agent Patrick O'Kain stated in an interview released on May 8, 2019, that Bitcoin now accounts for just 1% of money laundering activity, which is less than the percentage for the U.S. dollar.[175]

It's not hard to see why Bitcoin in its current form isn't very good for criminal activity. Because the Bitcoin blockchain contains every transaction in the history of the network, all a criminal investigator has to do is link an identity to a Bitcoin address at a single point in history and follow the transaction history from that point onward. "Chain analysis" has become an industry in its own right, with multiple companies using software to analyze the Bitcoin blockchain and provide corporate and government clients with actionable information that allows law enforcement to connect crimes with their perpetrators' identities. Meanwhile, as discussed in Chapter 8, money launderers continue to move $800 billion–$2 trillion annually through the normal banking system. Needless to say, the largest proportion of money laundering is believed to happen through the U.S. dollar.

Meanwhile, numerous agencies of the U.S. government have effectively accepted the legality of Bitcoin. The IRS has declared it "property" for purposes of levying income tax.[176] The Commodities Futures Trading Commission (CFTC) has deemed it a "commodity" and claimed jurisdiction with respect to trading it.[177] U.S. law enforcement services have auctioned bitcoins seized from criminals who acquired them via illegal activity.[178] In contrast to the treatment of illegal contraband, such as drugs, which must be destroyed if seized, the act of a government agency selling bitcoins is a stamp of approval with respect to their legality.

Risks to Fungibility

Fungibility is a risk for Bitcoin. In theory, a bitcoin is a bitcoin is a bitcoin. But the fact that it is often possible to tie an identity to a Bitcoin address means that if the identity is an enemy of the state, then governments can attempt to dissuade people from accepting payment from that address. For example, on November 28, 2018, the United States Treasury publicly identified two individuals, Ali Khorashadizadeh and Mohammad

Ghorbaniyan, as enablers of ransomware attacks using Bitcoin, and it blacklisted two particular Bitcoin addresses believed to be controlled by them.[179] It is possible that cases such as these could result in certain Bitcoin addresses being "tainted." This could result in a bifurcation of the Bitcoin system such that bitcoins in tainted or blacklisted addresses might only be able to circulate in the black market, while untainted ones circulate unhampered.

There is also the question of how long a Bitcoin remains tainted. In the world of dollars, once a $20 bill has been transacted five or six times subsequent to its theft, it becomes impossible to repossess it because by then multiple innocent parties in the economy will have used it legitimately. For example, a thief may steal some cash and pass it to his friend the money-launderer who puts it through the books of his restaurant. Then the restaurateur/money-launderer uses it to buy a book for his daughter. Then the bookstore owner uses the money to buy a turkey sandwich at the deli, and the deli owner pays the man working at the counter. If the police were to repossess the "stolen" money from the deli employee, he would rightly be dumbfounded. He didn't know anything about the theft that occurred four transactions prior.

It's possible that bitcoins are viewed differently since in theory anyone could search a government database to make sure the bitcoins they're planning to accept as payment for a good or service aren't stolen or even weren't stolen three or four transactions ago. It remains to be seen how this dynamic develops. One potential defense against such a development would be for Bitcoin users to deliberately interact with tainted addresses en masse. If enough Bitcoin enthusiasts were to swap bitcoins with tainted addresses, the pool of addresses might become so large that it becomes impractical for governments to attempt to blacklist so many people's funds. It is believed that roughly 90% of all $20 bills in circulation carry traces of cocaine,[180] which suggests that those bills were used to buy or at least consume cocaine at some point. Since the vast majority of twenties are thus tainted, nobody worries about somebody refusing to accept one of these bills as payment.

Taxation

I am not qualified as a tax advisor, and this should not be considered tax advice. Having made that statement, my impressions are as follows. It appears that the IRS issued guidance in 2014 that treats bitcoins as "property."[181] The bad news is that every transaction (including buying a good or service in exchange for bitcoins) could be considered a taxable event (with associated capital gains taxes due). You may be able to select which lots you sell, but you won't escape the tax unless you attempt to secretly evade income tax, which is not recommended.

Nevertheless, any cryptocurrency investor should assume that the rules will evolve and change as the sector grows. While it is prudent for investors to assume the worst in terms of tax treatment, there are proposals in the works to exempt taxation on Bitcoin for transactions below a certain threshold, say $600.[182] This would help facilitate its use as a medium of exchange, though such rule changes may not occur any time soon.

Central Bank Digital Currencies: Crypto Dollars, Euros, Yen, Yuan

Another concern that Bitcoin skeptics have raised is that current issuers of major world fiat currencies, including the dollar, euro, yen and yuan, could issue cryptocurrencies of their own to compete with Bitcoin. For example, a U.S. "Fedcoin" would likely take one of two forms. The first would be a dollar that, somewhat like Bitcoin, allows customers to use a private key to access a dollar deposit directly at the Fed. This type of cryptocurrency has the same potential flaw as that of the Narrow Bank discussed in Chapter 4. It could directly threaten the deposit-taking activities of the existing banking system. While the Narrow Bank could take market share from the existing banking system, Fedcoin could bypass the banking system altogether. If you can directly control your dollars without routing them through a bank, why bother with the bank? If a large portion of the populace were therefore to transfer their deposits out of the banking system and into fedcoins, the effects could be very negative for the banking system. Based on the Federal Reserve's pushback against the Narrow Bank, it seems unlikely that the Federal Reserve would imperil the banks this way anytime soon.

Another possible format would be a truly uncontrolled system (in which the Federal Reserve does not control the money supply). Such a currency might be able to compete with the existing dollar, but it would also obviate the need for the Federal Reserve! It seems extraordinarily unlikely that the Federal Reserve would voluntarily deprive itself of its own reason for existence. Ditto other central banks.

I think that neither of these possibilities is likely to occur soon. But if the Federal Reserve does eventually pursue one of these alternatives, it will be because Bitcoin has grown so large that it has effectively forced the Federal Reserve's hand. By that time, Bitcoin could be so widely adopted that it will be too late for the Federal Reserve to maintain the dollar's market share, even in cryptocurrency form.

Central Banks Return to Gold Standard

Another threat from government would be a credible return to a true gold standard or similar system. If the U.S. were to issue dollars that were 100% backed by gold, the U.S. dollar would become a much stronger currency. The probability of such an outcome is minuscule. It would eliminate active monetary policy, including the Federal Reserve's ability to set interest rates. It would limit the government's ability to deficit-spend and therefore curtail politicians' habit of delivering goodies to voters.

It would also be difficult to credibly execute. Since the U.S. government has already failed more than once to uphold a gold-backed dollar, citizens would rightly doubt its ability to pull off such a feat this time around. Even if the government were able to hold the peg to gold, Bitcoin would still be "harder" money due to gold's increase in supply of 1%–2% annually. For these various reasons, it appears extraordinarily unlikely that the U.S. or another major country will return to a gold standard or similar system that could credibly compete with Bitcoin.

Chapter 12

Economic Risks to Bitcoin

Economic risks are another major category of risks facing Bitcoin. This chapter will address the risks that are primarily economic in nature.

"Skinny" Bitcoin

Early Bitcoin investors recognized, as we described in the previous Chapter, that Bitcoin is both money and a software protocol, and specifically an *Internet* protocol. One of the key characteristics of the major Internet protocols that allowed them to spread so successfully was that they were open-source. Yet one economic shortcoming of the Internet has been that companies such as the Internet monopolists discussed earlier managed to capture the vast majority of the economic value in the Internet by taking those free and open source protocols and then building exclusive databases and services on top of them.

As articulated by venture capitalist Joel Monegro in his Fat Protocols[183] thesis, Bitcoin appears to be the first case of an Internet protocol where much of the value is captured within the protocol itself (in the value of bitcoins). This is not to say that the second layers and third layers described in Chapter 8 won't also capture value. I expect they will. Some people have argued that this time won't be different from the past, when the Internet protocols became commodities that captured no significant value. Ten years into Bitcoin's existence, it seems much more likely that Monegro is right and that Bitcoin will capture significant value.

Short-Term Price Volatility

Among the 14 Characteristics of Good Money, Bitcoin's weakest mark today is its Short-Term Stable Value. In the last eight years, Bitcoin's price has fallen by over 80% four separate times. This high level of volatility isn't surprising, given that most people haven't yet understood Bitcoin's upside potential, and the price is therefore subject to rapid changes in sentiment. This book is partly an attempt to help remedy that problem. However, there's no denying that the price volatility present in Bitcoin in its youth is a drawback, as it is with any "growth asset" (as described in Chapter 9). As with any investment, such volatility may tempt investors to try to "pick the bottom" in Bitcoin's price. Most who employ this tactic will fail. A risk-averse investor will therefore size any investment in Bitcoin appropriately and consider dollar-cost averaging over time in order to mitigate short-term risk of loss.

It's worth asking whether Bitcoin's short-term price volatility will ever fall to an acceptable level. As volatile as Bitcoin has been in recent years, it's less volatile than in its earlier years. This makes sense. The larger Bitcoin grows (in total value), the less its price gets pushed around by the marginal buyer or seller. Its existing market capitalization acts as ballast, and the bigger the total value, the more incremental change in demand is required to move the price a given percentage. However, since Bitcoin's supply is strictly limited, supply cannot respond to changes in demand. Every asset's price is a function of supply and demand. So, if supply is fixed, then small changes in demand get reflected dramatically in the price. This means that, all else being equal, Bitcoin's purchasing power will be more volatile than most other forms of money.

For example, if Bitcoin reaches a total value equal to that of the gold market (roughly $8 trillion), Bitcoin's price will still probably be more volatile than gold's price, since gold does not have a fixed supply and gold suppliers can respond (albeit modestly) to changes in demand. I can imagine a scenario in which Bitcoin becomes so massive (say $50 trillion of total value) that its price volatility is reduced. But even if all goes well for Bitcoin, that point is probably two decades away or more. The bottom line is that we should assume that Bitcoin will for a long time be more short-term volatile than strong fiat currencies like the dollar.

Market Manipulation

All asset prices are manipulated to some degree. This includes major monetary metals such as gold. Considering that Bitcoin is still a nascent asset, its price (in terms of dollars) may be subject to greater manipulation than is the case with more mature assets. The manipulation issue has been brought into stark relief by the efforts of several companies to bring to market a Bitcoin exchange-traded fund (ETF).

In a letter published January 18, 2018, Dalia Blass, the Director of the Securities Exchange Commission (SEC)'s Division of Investment Management, identified five key hurdles for the development of crypto-based ETFs or mutual funds: (1) valuation, (2) liquidity, (3) custody, (4) arbitrage, and (5) manipulation.[184] The message to financial markets at that time was essentially "hold your horses, folks; there are a lot of issues to resolve before we can support an ETF product." Since that time, it appears that issues 1–4 listed above have been solved or are likely to be solved soon. The hardest issue is (5) manipulation.

However, since that time the major U.S.-based exchanges that account for a significant portion of global Bitcoin trading volume have implemented market surveillance systems that allow for the recognition, tracking, and mitigation of suspect trading activities. Bitwise Asset Management (a company that has one of the Bitcoin ETF applications on file with the SEC) presented data on March 20, 2019, that highlighted how efficient the Bitcoin market is globally, especially with respect to liquidity and the tightness of bid/ask spreads on major U.S. Bitcoin exchanges.185 Although manipulation can never be reduced to zero, it seems likely that manipulation in the Bitcoin market will be brought into line with manipulation in other major assets eventually.

Satoshi's Stash

Although nobody knows for sure, quite a few people believe that Bitcoin's creator, the pseudonymous "Satoshi Nakamoto," owns a lot of bitcoins, possibly as much as 5% of the total 21 million.[186] This makes sense considering that he/she/they were the only ones supporting the network in the first year or so. Satoshi clearly went to great lengths to protect anonymity. However, it's possible that Satoshi could eventually be unmasked or that Satoshi could spend his/her/their coins, which have been sitting motionless for years. I believe that Satoshi's fading into the mist has been good for the Bitcoin ecosystem, and if Satoshi were to re-emerge or spend those bitcoins, it would be negative for the price of bitcoins and the Bitcoin network overall.

Another concern surrounds Satoshi's pseudonymity in general. When I first researched Bitcoin, I was worried that this shadowy character could be a scammer. Over time I realized that the founder's pseudonymity is a feature, not a bug. The benefit is enhanced decentralization. If Satoshi's identity were to be revealed, the hero-worship that would be associated with such a revelation could lead to Satoshi having excessive influence over the network and the community. Since Bitcoin's strength lies in its decentralization, it's better not to have an active founder/leader.

I can also understand why Satoshi has protected his/her/their pseudonymity considering the history of governments attacking centralized systems for money, including E-gold, which was a non-governmental gold-backed monetary system that was ultimately shut down by the government.[187] It is due to the threat of government reaction to a competing currency that Nobel Prize–winning Austrian school economist Friedrich Hayek stated in a 1984 interview, "I don't believe we shall ever have a good money again before we take the thing out of the hands of government; that is, we can't take them violently out of the hands of government, all we can do is by some sly roundabout way introduce something that they can't stop."[188] Maintaining pseudonymity seems to be just the "sly roundabout way" to introduce and maintain a competing currency like Bitcoin.

Another complaint that some people have about Satoshi's pseudonymity is their fear of a "kill switch" or "back door" in the code that could allow the creator to either deactivate the system or steal from it. As discussed earlier, the fact that Bitcoin's software is open-source and has been crawled over by thousands or tens of thousands of software developers and hackers means the chance that there is some undiscovered secret kill switch or back door is near-zero.

Cryptocurrency Competition from the Internet Monopolists

Everyone living on planet Earth should worry about whether Jeff Bezos is coming after their company, industry, profession, or livelihood. Amazon has demonstrated a willingness to make big and risky bets on numerous industries and products, and a Bitcoin-like cryptocurrency would certainly be within Amazon's skill set. Bitcoin is Internet-based and requires large amounts of computational capacity. Amazon understands both of these areas very well, especially due to its cloud services business, in which it is believed to have roughly a third of global market share.[189]

At first glance, it's surprising that Amazon hasn't already launched a competitive cryptocurrency. With every credit card sale it makes on its website, Amazon loses percentage points of revenue to the credit card processors. All Amazon would have to do to recapture some of that lost margin would be to launch a new "Bezosbucks" cryptocurrency. Amazon might achieve near-instant adoption of Bezosbucks by tens of millions of people since the high-volume subset of Amazon's customer base, represented by its Amazon Prime membership list, exceeds 100 million people.[190]

With roughly 2.4 billion active users,[191] Facebook has an even bigger user base than Amazon, and Facebook has announced its intent to launch both a semi-decentralized cryptocurrency called "Libra" and a "wallet" system that will allow transfer of this currency.[192] The proposed system is creative and potentially very profitable for Facebook. As proposed, the system is a partially decentralized consortium. Facebook has already lined up 28 different organizations, including Visa, Mastercard, eBay, Spotify, Uber, and Vodafone, and aims to increase the number of consortium members to 100 by the target launch date in the first half of 2020. The new cryptocurrency is designed initially as a "stablecoin" that would have far less short-term price volatility than Bitcoin, at least until Bitcoin gains much wider adoption.

In some respects, it's shocking that Facebook has taken so long to launch its own payment system. The two largest non-American Internet giants, Tencent and Alibaba, have built huge businesses in peer-to-peer payments via their WeChat Pay and Alipay apps. Between them they have split the payments business in China almost 50/50 into a cozy duopoly.[193] Facebook therefore appears to simply be following in the footsteps of other very successful social network and Internet-native companies with respect to getting into the payments game.

Governments (not just China's) love this sort of outcome because it allows for close surveillance of payments. However, Facebook's proposed plan is more audacious than the WeChat Pay and Alipay systems because it does not rely exclusively on its domestic national currency. Its use of a basket of multiple assets poses an explicit long-term challenge to the U.S. dollar and an even greater threat to weaker fiat currencies, especially those of some developing countries. Moreover, the set of assets backing the currency will include interest-bearing bank accounts and government securities. This implies that Libra will function like a money market fund, but with shares that can be transferred among different users. However, instead of the currency holders collecting the interest on the basket of assets, the returns will accrue to the consortium backing it. Consortium members will pay $10 million each to operate a node and vote in the governance of the system.

The organization has stated that "An important objective of the Libra Association is to move toward increasing decentralization over time... As discussed above, the association will develop a path toward permission-less governance and consensus on the Libra network. The association's objective will be to start this transition within five years."[194] Considering the audacious goal of creating a payment system based on a *brand-new currency* and given Facebook's poor track record with respect to public trust in recent years, it's not surprising that government is already pushing back. On June 18, 2018, Congresswoman and Chairwoman of the House Financial Services Committee Maxine Waters issued a statement "requesting that Facebook agree to a moratorium on any movement forward on developing a cryptocurrency until Congress and regulators have the opportunity to examine these issues and take action."[195]

I expect plenty of government pushback against Facebook's new currency, which will appear to some to be an aggressive attempt to reach deeper into the lives of its users. It's too early to know how this will play out, but if Libra does end up launching—an outcome that I put at about 50% probability—it will most likely be (1) censorable, (2) seizable, (3) unlimited supply (non-scarce), and (4) fully surveilled (non-private). Discussions of such a currency competing with Bitcoin are a little like discussions of a boat competing with a car. They're both modes of transportation, but they're so different from each other that they solve completely different problems. I personally think that Libra will *accelerate* adoption of Bitcoin because some portion of Facebook's 2.4 billion active users globally that were either skeptical or ignorant of Bitcoin will be introduced to a "cryptocurrency," adopt it, and then learn why an actual (scarce, unseizable, censorship-resistant) cryptocurrency like Bitcoin is so much better than Facebook's product.

Both Amazon and Facebook have had ample opportunity to launch their own cryptocurrency products. Bitcoin has been known to portions of the tech-savvy public for years. Amazon's and Facebook's strategy teams have probably waited this long because of some significant potential drawbacks. Perhaps the most obvious are politics and government scrutiny. President Trump managed to catch the populist wave of disenfranchised people who have seen their living standards fall in recent decades as their jobs disappeared. He apparently managed to convince a portion of his supporters that it was offshoring and immigration that took those jobs. Once these folks realize that the *current* primary driver is actually technology via automation (robotics, artificial intelligence), the substitution of online sales channels (Amazon) for physical stores that employ people, and the gig economy, the tech giants are likely to face much more political and regulatory heat. Some presidential candidates are already talking about going far beyond hitting them with fines as the Europeans have already done. The possibility of regulating or even breaking up these Internet monopolists is now being discussed.[196]

Additionally, although profit margins at U.S. companies have remained much higher than the long-term average for many years, it has taken a long time for people to realize that consolidation and monopoly behavior have reached near-record highs not seen for at least half a century and possibly since the Gilded Age over a century ago.[197] The Democratic Party is finally focusing on this issue, and voters will be paying attention in the next election. This struggle could take years to play out, but Bezos and Zuckerberg are known to play the long game, and these dynamics will surely shape their strategies.

The European regulators have already been working for years to contain the Internet monopolists. Witness the multiple fines levied against Google totaling over *$9 billion*.[198] I expect such actions to eventually come from the United States government also, whether in the form of much more serious fines than have been leveled or in more substantial regulatory action, though they may have to wait until a Democratic administration. So the Internet monopolists must decide whether they want to bring additional scrutiny to themselves and risk adding to the tech industry's history yet another case of using market power (via distribution through their huge online sales channels) to attempt to launch a new product (a "cryptocurrency") that may increase government scrutiny on their overall activities. To a competent regulator, an Internet monopolist launching its own currency could look a lot like (1) Microsoft's successful attempt in the 1990s to take the Internet browser market away from Netscape by bundling Internet Explorer with Windows, or (2) Google's prioritizing of its own shopping services in its search results (for which it recently received a multi-billion-dollar fine from the EU).[199] Amazon may have concluded that so far it's not worth the potential political and regulatory backlash.

The risk of one of the Internet monopolists attempting to compete with Bitcoin reminds me of a trade I made back in 2012 in Netflix stock. Netflix had recently been "Amazoned" when Amazon launched its competing online video service. Netflix had also been "Comcasted" and "Hulued" (both companies had announced expanded video services). Then, compounding its problems, Netflix lost one of its major sources of content when Starz refused to renew its contract. In one year (summer 2011—summer 2012) Netflix stock fell by almost 80%.

I decided to take a flyer on it. I didn't think the company would die. I bought 1,000 shares at about $60 per share. A few months later the stock traded up to $90 and I sold it. I made a 50% gain and $30,000 pre-tax profit in the span of a few months. Not a bad trade, right? Wrong. If I had held that investment until today (almost seven years), my $60,000 would now be worth roughly *$2.4 million*. Would I have held it all the way up? No, I would have trimmed the position along the way. Nevertheless, selling Netflix when I did was the worst trade of my life so far.

Every investor who's been at the game for at least a decade has one of these stories, but what makes this one salient to Bitcoin is that it involved the misunderstanding of network effects' potential for investment upside. The reason Netflix is as valuable as it is now is that the user base is global and growing, and the more users there are, the more Netflix can spend on good content, and the more valuable the content, the more users join the system. This feedback loop creates a network effect. Moreover, Netflix benefits directly from advances in bandwidth, storage, and computation that power the Internet. It is Internet-native. Does this sound familiar? The same factors apply for Bitcoin.

So what did I miss seven years ago when I sold my Netflix stock for a measly 50% gain? At the time, I hadn't realized that network effects would apply to Netflix. And I also didn't realize that in the game of network effects, being the first to get to scale is crucial. Can a latecomer unseat the first mover if the latecomer is backed by a big enough player? Yes, but it's tough.

Facebook managed to unseat Myspace because Facebook arrived early enough and had a better product. But later, Google tried to catch Facebook with its social networking product and failed, despite having over $200 billion of market capitalization and some of the world's best software talent behind the effort. Do you know what Google's social network is called? Me neither. Facebook managed to get to scale in time to repel an attack by Google, one of the strongest companies in the world.

With over 10 years of dominance in the cryptocurrency market, time is getting late for potential Bitcoin competitors to catch up. Moreover, any "cryptocurrency" launched by the Internet monopolists risks regulatory backlash. And it will also be unattractive to users who want to put their money into a cryptocurrency that can't easily be controlled. I have learned from my Netflix mistake, and I'm not going to miss an attractive chance to buy into a network effect–driven investment like Bitcoin.

Chapter 13

Sociological and Psychological Risks to Bitcoin

I have labeled the last major category of risks facing Bitcoin as "sociological and psychological." They reflect issues associated with social and perceptual dynamics of both individuals and groups of people.

Naysayers and the Media

The list of high-profile naysayers who have labeled Bitcoin a scam is almost as long as the list of news articles that have declared Bitcoin dead. For the latter, see https://99bitcoins.com/bitcoin-obituaries, which lists hundreds of articles and reports on the impending or actual death of Bitcoin. Notwithstanding these obituaries, as of this writing Bitcoin is still not dead. On the contrary; it appears to be in rude health.

In every such case of greatly exaggerated pronouncements of the death of Bitcoin, you must remember the incentives and motivations of the naysayer or obituary writer. In the case of the news media, there appears to be an overwhelming incentive to publish sensational clickbait stories that "trigger" the reader's emotions. That's because emotional activation is what drives engagement and therefore advertising revenue. Unfortunately, in a world of monopolist platforms (Facebook, Google) that serve as gatekeepers for people's valuable attention, journalists face powerful pressures to grab that attention by any means necessary. Monetizing eyeballs and user engagement is the game. Like politicians who face an inexorable pressure to spend, many journalists are forced to pander to the system in order to stay employed.

In the case of high-profile naysayers, incentives and motivations are also crucial. The sad truth is that the majority of economically powerful people have a huge stake in the existing dysfunctional system. Of course Jamie Dimon has called Bitcoin a fraud. He is the CEO of the largest western bank in the world—one of the banks that has so ably captured its own regulators and managed to extract rents from the economy while getting ever larger and too-big-to-fail such that it benefits from the full backing of the United States government. Of course Warren Buffett and Charlie Munger have said bad things about Bitcoin. As of December 31, 2018, their primary investment vehicle, Berkshire Hathaway, owned over $40 billion of Bank of America and Wells Fargo stock.[200]

These bankers and bank investors with huge vested interests in the existing monetary system "protest too much" about Bitcoin because they are at risk of losing immense profits if Bitcoin reaches mass adoption. Bitcoin threatens the banks' core businesses of (1) payment processing, (2) cash management, (3) capital raising, (4) credit allocation (lending), and (5) data selling. (Yes, the banks sell your personal spending data whether you like it or not, just as Facebook and Google do.)[201] In the banking sector, tens of billions of dollars of annual profits and hundreds of billions of dollars of bank market capitalization are at stake. Bankers and bank investors realize that the network effect dynamic of Bitcoin (as with all currencies) means that the more that people adopt it, the more people will want to adopt it. Given Bitcoin's lead, launching a competing cryptocurrency is unlikely to dampen demand for Bitcoin. So the primary remaining tool available to them is shouting it down. Fortunately, this tactic is unlikely to succeed.

Another interesting case is Howard Marks, who founded Oaktree Capital, one of the largest investment firms in my hometown of Los Angeles. Marks is well-respected in the investment community, and several times a year he publishes a memo with his thoughts on the investment landscape. In July 2017 he published a memo in which he dismissed Bitcoin as "a fad."[202] Then two months later he recanted and published another memo in which he admitted he hadn't understood Bitcoin.[203] I applaud Marks' candor and admission of error. He is more honest than most, though his honesty is less surprising since his business may be less threatened than those of others in the financial world such as the banks. We must always ask ourselves about the motivation of the person offering the opinion about Bitcoin. Unless and until Bitcoin is pervasive and unavoidable, no senior employee of any commercial bank, credit card processor, or remittance processor can come out in favor of Bitcoin, because their core businesses are too threatened by it.

"Better" Bitcoins

This book has focused on Bitcoin and has largely neglected other cryptocurrencies. This was done primarily because Bitcoin stands head and shoulders above the rest of the existing cryptocurrencies. Bitcoin is the clear leader and has the best chance of competing with existing monies like the dollar and gold. It has the strongest brand. It has the longest track record of proven success and security. It has a story of "immaculate conception" due to its release into the world by its pseudonymous creator. It has the strongest network effect. It has the most computational resources dedicated to securing its network. These factors are probably impossible to replicate.

Bitcoin's history of success since inception makes it the most "Lindy" cryptocurrency out there. As articulated by Albert Goldman in 1964,[204] Benoit Mandelbrot in the 1983,[205] and Nassim Taleb in 2012,[206] the Lindy Effect is the phenomenon whereby the life expectancy of a nonperishable thing like an idea or technology *increases with age*. The origin of the term is Lindy's eatery in New York, where actors and critics would congregate and discuss the prospects of shows currently running on Broadway. It was observed that the longer a show had been running, the longer it was likely to keep running. As applied to ideas/technologies, the longer an idea/technology survives without perishing, the longer it is expected to survive in the future. That's because the longer something's track record of surviving challenges and attacks, the more confident we can be that it will persist into the future. Things that are Lindy have "stood the test of time."

One of the key reasons I bought Bitcoin is that it had already been a multi-hundred-million-dollar and then billion-dollar hacking target for years and yet the network hadn't been compromised even once. This meant it was battle-hardened and evidently quite secure. I can envision scenarios in which Bitcoin fails and one of the other cryptocurrencies succeeds. This could happen due to Bitcoin failing to scale or Bitcoin's proof of work–based "Nakamoto Consensus" mechanism failing while another consensus mechanism succeeds. Or it could be due to powerful actors such as governments acting in concert to attack Bitcoin while supporting an alternative. It's also possible that several cryptocurrencies with very different characteristics can coexist and thrive because they solve different problems. The future is not yet written, and although Bitcoin is the clear leader, it might not ultimately be the "winner who takes all." But unseating Bitcoin is a very tall order, and it seems the risk of Bitcoin losing its crown is rather small.

The Bitcoin Fever Already Peaked

One of the more ridiculous Bitcoin-related arguments I've seen was put forth by the British bank Barclays in April 2018. The bank modeled cryptocurrency adoption as an infectious disease epidemic and suggested that the disease had already reached anyone who might be susceptible. It further suggested a "generous upper bound" for the value of the entire cryptocurrency market (including Bitcoin) of $780 billion.[207] I believe this statement is likely to go down in history next to Paul Krugman's comment mentioned in the Preface to this book that "by 2005 or so it will become clear that the Internet's impact on the economy has been no greater than the fax machine's."

The infectious disease model is flawed for three reasons. First, exposure to Bitcoin of 2018 is not the same as exposure to Bitcoin of 2020 because, as discussed earlier, Bitcoin is constantly improving as the developers upgrade the code and the miners deploy more security-enhancing mining capacity (hash power). Second, the global debt problem, with its associated risks of financial repression (low and negative interest rates) and inflation, grows continuously. So the need for an inflation-resistant (scarce) asset increases by the day.

Third, "exposure" to Bitcoin is not the same as exposure to an infectious disease. As discussed in this book's Preface, I was "exposed" to Bitcoin in 2013, and then exposed again in 2016, but I didn't "catch the disease" either time. Only when I really did my research in 2017 did the "infection" take hold. Since then my affliction has indeed worsened dramatically and I expect it to be chronic. A single exposure, however, is not enough to infect someone with the Bitcoin disease. Only education and research—of the kind that requires repeated exposures to the subject matter, including through reading books like this one—can do that. Most people on this planet have not yet truly been exposed. Unless Bitcoin actually fails, expect to find me doing my part to expose them.

The Technological Generational Gap (Bitcoin for Boomers)

On average, it will take longer for retirees to understand the benefits of Bitcoin than for younger people. It took about two decades for the general public to realize the value of the major Internet companies. Bitcoin has been around for over a decade, which suggests another decade to reach widespread recognition based on a similar timeline. However, there is ample evidence that adoption curves for new technology have been shortening over time. Televisions were adopted more quickly than automobiles. Personal computers were adopted more quickly than televisions. Smartphones were adopted more quickly than personal computers.[208] The current adoption rate of Bitcoin, which has already seen orders of magnitude gains in both price and usership over multiple boom/bust cycles, seems pretty rapid.

Even if seniors don't adopt Bitcoin in significant size, time (as with all demographic-based demand issues) is on the side of the youngsters. A survey of over 2,000 American adults conducted by Harris Poll on April 23-15, 2019, concluded that among those aged 18–34, 60% described themselves as at least "somewhat familiar" with Bitcoin. Among those age 65 and over, just 20% were. When asked whether they agreed with the statement that "Bitcoin is a positive innovation in financial technology," 59% of the 18–34 cohort agreed, while just 24% of the over-65 cohort did. When asked whether they agreed with the statement "it's likely most people will be using Bitcoin in the next 10 years," 48% of those aged 18–34 "strongly" agreed or "somewhat" agreed, while the figure was just 16% for the over-65s. Most importantly, the percentage of people that indicated they were "very" or "somewhat" likely to buy

Bitcoin in the next five years was 42% among the 18–34 cohort and just 8% among the over-65 cohort.[209]

Nobel Prize–winning quantum physicist Max Planck is credited with saying that "a new scientific truth does not triumph by convincing its opponents and making them see the light, but rather because its opponents eventually die, and a new generation grows up that is familiar with it."[210] Fortunately for Bitcoin, investment reallocation happens much more quickly than generational die-offs do. That's because young and middle-aged people invest while old people divest. The over-65 cohort is, on average, spending down wealth accumulated earlier in life. Conversely, the 18–34 cohort is just entering the asset accumulation phase. Asset prices are set at the margin, and the investment behavior of this young cohort will set the direction for asset price movements in the coming decades. As the millennial cohort saves and invests its wealth, this incremental demand is likely to increase the portion of overall global asset value allocated to Bitcoin. Millennials will likely decide they want to put some portion of their portfolios in an asset class that is inflation-proof and uncorrelated to other risk assets.

Are these young citizens of the Internet going to plump for something that is portable, can function as a medium of exchange, and has the option of being stored online, on-premise, in a vault, or in their brains? Or are they going to choose the shiny metal and the green paper? If you are not a member of the younger generation, you should quiz your kids, grandkids, nieces, or nephews about this. Their answers might surprise you.

The Environment and the World's First Global Market for Energy

Another criticism commonly leveled against Bitcoin concerns its energy usage. Bitcoin does consume a lot of electricity, and since Bitcoin is a global, decentralized network of computers with an amalgam of different mining machines operating at different efficiency levels and different costs of energy, it's difficult to even come up with a realistic estimate of the system's total energy usage. The precision of such an estimate might be limited to an order of magnitude. As time passes and the network's security increases, the energy cost will likely continue to rise even as the mining equipment becomes more efficient. This has some environmentalists up in arms.

We should approach the energy usage for Bitcoin the same way we approach energy usage for any other application. If people value the service it provides, they will expend resources on it. Bitcoin's energy usage is 100% driven by demand. The network operators (miners) use electricity to secure the network in order to earn bitcoins and transaction fees. If the non-miner population on Earth didn't value bitcoins, their price would plummet to zero, miners would stop running their computers, and the energy usage would disappear. So energy usage by the Bitcoin network is simply an indication that people value bitcoins, just as energy usage in transportation indicates that people value travel, and energy usage in the home shows that people value turning on their lights at night.

As with all uses of energy, the way Bitcoin's energy usage can go wrong is with respect to the *source* of energy it uses. The same is true for transportation, lighting, and every other human use of energy. If the world runs on clean energy that produces little or no carbon emissions, other greenhouse gases, or pollutants, then all is well. If instead the world runs on burning dirty coal, then we can have problems, including potential climate change and particulate air pollution. It's no different with Bitcoin.

So people who care about the environment (a group that includes me) should think carefully when considering the impact of Bitcoin's energy usage and comparing it with other systems. For example, when comparing Bitcoin to the U.S. dollar, you have to consider the costs of printing dollars, distributing them securely to the banking system, maintaining a bank branch system (including all the attendant energy and personnel costs), running customer websites (and associated data centers), etc. All those costs are substantial, but they are probably dwarfed by the biggest cost of supporting the U.S. dollar: the military.

The United States military budget for 2019 was $686 billion.[211] One of the uses of this military might is the support for the dollar as global reserve currency. This is the manifestation of one of the 14 Characteristics of Good Money discussed earlier: being backed by a powerful agent. It's no coincidence that (1) the vast majority of oil contracts are denominated in U.S. dollars, and (2) the U.S. has mounted multiple expeditionary military efforts in the Middle East over multiple decades. This military power includes homeland security and local police forces. If you doubt the importance of this military backing, ask yourself what would happen to the value of the U.S. dollar if the government lost its physical power to punish tax evaders. So it's reasonable to ask how much energy is consumed in supporting the U.S. military, which, in turn, supports the U.S. dollar. I don't know how to quantify the energy usage of the U.S. military, but I'd bet that it's huge.

The Bitcoin network's energy usage has some interesting characteristics that argue in favor of its ultimate impact on the environment. Because energy is the primary variable cost input to running a Bitcoin mining operation, there exists a huge incentive for miners to access the cheapest source of electricity available. When bitcoins are trading for $8,500 apiece, accessing cheap electricity can mean the difference between booking a net profit of $2,000 per bitcoin mined or making no profit at all. Taking into account the capital cost of the computers, a mining operation with access to very cheap electricity can be very profitable, while one that uses more expensive electricity generates losses.

While electricity is the primary mode for energy consumption globally, it has always suffered from one major shortcoming: long-distance distribution. Although the United States has a well-developed power grid with significant interconnections across the country, its energy market is still fragmented. A key reason is that electricity can't be transported across wires for hundreds of miles without significant energy loss. This means that environmentally sound sources of energy like wind farms, solar farms, or hydroelectric dams that are located in remote areas can only support energy consumption of local populations or industries. Although many of these generation facilities can produce energy far in excess of what can be used locally, any surplus generation beyond the needs of local consumers is wasted.

Initial clues about potential solutions to this problem have been illustrated by The Dalles in Oregon.[212] Google and Facebook have built giant data centers in The Dalles next to cheap, clean hydroelectric power generated by the mighty Columbia River in Oregon. This location is somewhat remote from major population centers. However, one of the interesting lessons of the evolution of cloud computing and computation on the Internet is that you can't make everything remote. Netflix can't just build a giant server farm in some isolated area in the middle of the United States in order to remotely serve all of its video-streaming clients in cities across America.

That's because streaming video over long distances results in "latency" (delays in transmission that cause a poor user experience). The same is true for Google's search algorithm that we all use every day. That nifty Google search auto-complete function that suggests what you're looking for before you can even finish typing it can't live in a data center a thousand miles away. In order to provide answers fast, that server has to be closer to your personal computer or cell phone.

Bitcoin is different. Bitcoin provides a way for remote electricity-producing assets to be put to effective use. Although Bitcoin miners do require Internet access, they are not nearly as sensitive to network speed and latency as Google and Netflix are. This means that remote energy sources that are too far from population centers for major data center users requiring low latency can instead be used by Bitcoin miners.

Another interesting element is the cost of this energy. Remote-located wind farms, solar farms, and hydroelectric plants have extraordinarily low marginal production costs. In the case of hydroelectric, it's near zero. Also, these types of energy are among the cleanest (in terms of greenhouse gas production and air pollution). So, while data are sketchy at this point, there is some evidence that the majority of energy used to support the Bitcoin network is clean energy.[213] Research in this area is ongoing, and the topography of the network is evolving rapidly. Because Bitcoin miners seek the cheapest sources of electricity, and many of the cheapest sources are also the cleanest, Bitcoin has in some sense created the first global market for electricity. Now any source of electricity, including remote but clean hydroelectric dams, wind farms, and solar arrays can be used to mine Bitcoin when local demand from other populations and industries falls short.

Bitcoin has also found a way to mitigate some of the effects of one of the worst greenhouse gas offenders: the oil and gas industry. Oil drillers frequently encounter and pump hydrocarbons other than crude oil as a byproduct of their drilling activities. One of these major byproducts is natural gas. Overall, if properly handled and consumed, natural gas is significantly cleaner than coal or oil. However, one of the most notorious practices in the entire energy industry is the oil and gas drilling industry's practice of "flaring." In cases in which oil drillers can't economically transport the natural gas they collect, they sometimes just burn their excess production, releasing earth-warming greenhouse gases into the atmosphere.[214] Worse, the overall natural gas production, transport, and storage system is highly prone to leaks.[215] According to the influential scientific journal *Nature*, natural gas (primarily methane) has a significantly worse long-term effect on climate change than carbon dioxide; it is potentially 25x more potent.[216] This means that leaked natural gas can be even more destructive long-term than flared natural gas.

Bitcoin has brought an interesting solution to the problem. A company called Upstream Data delivers Bitcoin mining "skids" (modular containers holding Bitcoin mining equipment) to well heads with excess natural gas that the drillers would otherwise flare or leak. Instead, the excess gas can be used to mine Bitcoin.[217] This reduces greenhouse gas emissions, provides revenue for natural gas producers, and supports the world's biggest open financial system.

Pyramids and Ponzis

Some folks have argued that Bitcoin is a pyramid scheme. That's true in one important respect, which is that if you buy Bitcoin early and if more people buy it later, then you will benefit financially from their purchases. That's because the supply is strictly limited, and an increase in demand moves the price upward as more people buy in. Furthermore, this creates an incentive for you to pitch other people on the virtues of the asset so that they buy in.

However, this incentive structure is true of any limited-supply asset whose potential has not yet been fully realized. No rational investors bought Amazon stock in 2003 because they were excited to collect nice dividends the following quarter. Amazon wasn't paying dividends or even generating cash flow. Investors bought Amazon because they expected it to generate cash flow someday in the future *once its growth potential had been realized*. Bitcoin is similar. As discussed in Chapter 10, Bitcoin is still a juvenile in development. If you don't think that Bitcoin has room for improvement (including through novel uses for programmable digital money, and direct improvements to usability being built on top of it, such as the Lightning Network), then you should be much less interested in owning it, all else being equal.

Bitcoin also has an important feedback loop mechanism that actually improves its value just from people buying it and driving up its price. The higher the price, the more profit miners can make. This induces existing or new miners to bring more computational resources to the network. This increase in mining hash power increases the security of the network and makes attacking it more difficult. Greater network security implies that network should be more valuable as a system for storing or transmitting value. This positive feedback loop means that more people buying Bitcoin actually makes it more secure and therefore makes it more valuable. Moreover, the more people that own Bitcoin, the more likely it is to be used as the medium of exchange it was intended to be because its "network effect" is improved. If I have bitcoins and you have bitcoins, we both speak the same Bitcoin language. Maybe if I sell you a good or service, you pay me with bitcoins or vice versa.

Some people have called Bitcoin a Ponzi scheme. In a Ponzi scheme, new participants fund the payouts of earlier participants based on a promised or reported investment return that exceeds the investment return actually realized. For example, if someone (such as Bernie Madoff) takes investor funds and either reports or promises a 10% annualized return while only achieving a 5% return, then the claims on assets now exceed the actual assets available to satisfy the claims. The only thing that can keep the scheme going is to bring in more money to pay the existing claims. Bitcoin is *not* a Ponzi scheme because the rate of return is fully transparent to the users. Indeed, since it is opensource, the entire software and ledger of ownership is fully transparent to the entire world.

Fringe Status as an Investment

Bitcoin is still considered a "fringe" investment, but this is changing quickly. The latest evidence of the "mainstreaming" of Bitcoin as an investment is apparent in the actions of major financial markets participants such as Intercontinental Exchange and Fidelity. On August 3, 2018, Intercontinental Exchange (NYSE ticker "ICE") announced its plans to launch Bakkt, an "integrated platform to enable both consumers and institutions to buy, sell, store, and spend digital assets."[218] The announcement was accompanied by a feature article by *Fortune* magazine entitled "The NYSE's Owner Wants to Bring Bitcoin to Your 401(k). Are Crypto Credit Cards Next?"[219]

Intercontinental Exchange has a market capitalization in excess of $40 billion, which makes it the world's most valuable securities exchange and clearinghouse enterprise. It owns the New York Stock Exchange (NYSE) and other major exchanges and clearinghouses. In short, it is the Godzilla of the exchange world. This means that a large portion of the existing global institutional investor community already has links to its platform. ICE's new Bitcoin system will include both (1) regulated custody, and (2) regulated exchange. These are, in my opinion, the final missing pieces for institutional investors to get involved in crypto in a significant way. ICE had already been secretly developing the platform for 14 months in "stealth mode" before announcing it, and the platform is expected to go live in 2019. The project's official backers include Boston Consulting Group, Microsoft, and Starbucks, which wants to enable Bitcoin payments at its giant coffee store chain.

Almost as momentous as the Intercontinental Exchange announcement was Fidelity's announcement that it would provide an order routing service and institutional-grade custodial service for crypto.[220] With $2.4 trillion of assets under management and $6.8 trillion of assets under administration, Fidelity ranks among the largest asset managers on Earth.[221] This investment stalwart's participation in the Bitcoin market is a strong indication of Bitcoin's mainstreaming. Considering that Fidelity is one of the largest 401(k) retirement plan providers in the world, I foresee a scenario in which Fidelity offers a Bitcoin product within its 401(k) accounts. Such a product would open up a huge channel into Bitcoin.

On May 2, 2019, Fidelity announced the results of a survey it commissioned from Greenwich Associates. The survey, which included over 400 U.S. institutional investors, indicated that 22% of institutional investors already have some exposure to digital assets.[222,223] I suspect this result is significantly overstated, possibly due to selection bias among participants because Bitcoin enthusiasts are more likely to respond to a survey like this. Nevertheless, if the true level of institutional adoption is even half of the 22% reported level, that would still imply a double-digit percentage of the market. That would be a very significant participation level for institutional money already.

Unknown Unknowns

In its decade-plus of existence, Bitcoin has already surmounted numerous challenges, including a schism that resulted in a "hard fork" mentioned earlier that occurred in August 2017. Thus far, the system's governance structure of checks and balances among the various stakeholders has generally proven resilient. Granted, a decade is far shorter than the track record of many resilient systems that we now take for granted. But "Internet years" are similar to "dog years." A decade on the Internet is a very long time, and any Internet-native phenomenon that survives that long probably has something special. Very likely it has a network effect that is durable.

As with any investment, we must concede the possibility that some threat we haven't thought of impairs the functioning, and therefore the value, of Bitcoin. However, I think that we have likely covered most or all of the potential threats to Bitcoin in this book. To my mind, Bitcoin's potential upside as an investment far outweighs the risks.

Conclusion

I believe that the primary mistake people make when they dismiss or ignore Bitcoin is failing to do the work to understand it. In Bitcoin's first decade, this wasn't their fault. After all, a major new form of money doesn't come around very often, and most people haven't been provided with a basic framework like the 14 Characteristics of Good Money. I hope this book has provided you with some basics on the characteristics of good money, the indebted state of the financial system, Bitcoin's basic mechanics, Bitcoin's potential, and Bitcoin's risks. When Bitcoin was born mysteriously into the world as if by immaculate conception, it was a moonshot. Somewhat like a start-up company, but really more like a new software protocol, Bitcoin faced very long odds.

Having survived and then thrived in its first decade of life, Bitcoin's outlook is now much less tenuous. With millions of Bitcoin holders globally, as well as thousands of software developers, hardware developers, entrepreneurs, academics, and educators supporting the network, it's not surprising that Bitcoin has significantly narrowed the gap between zero and global currency status. Undoubtedly there are things that could kill Bitcoin. Yet Bitcoin has already survived four boom and bust cycles in which it has lost over 80% of its value, and with each cycle it rises to a new high. This last cycle has left it with a market value of roughly $150 billion.

I still encounter people who view Bitcoin as a start-up. But with over ten years of battle under its belt, Bitcoin has developed well past infancy. A decade from now it will have passed through adolescence and reached adulthood. Those who weren't paying attention will have missed both a fascinating journey and possibly the best investment opportunity of their lives. It's not too late to discover the possibilities of Bitcoin. If you've read this far, you've already begun your journey. I encourage you to travel onward!

About the Author

Andy Edstrom, CFA, CFP, is a financial advisor and a member of the investment committee at WESCAP Group, where he manages wealth and provides financial advice to clients. His opinions on Bitcoin have been published in *The Wall Street Journal*, and his opinions on regulation of the Internet monopolies have been published in *The Economist*.

Prior to joining WESCAP Group, Andy was a professional investor at a hedge fund and a private equity fund. Before the Global Financial Crisis of 2008–2009, he caught a glimpse into the making of "financial sausage" while working at Goldman Sachs.

Andy holds the Chartered Financial Analyst (CFA®) and Certified Financial Planner (CFP®) credentials, as well as a Bachelor of Arts in Economics, Magna Cum Laude and Phi Beta Kappa, from Williams College.

Acknowledgments

This book benefited greatly from Beth Rashbaum, whose expert editing clarified the book's message. Matt Phair provided valuable comments, especially on issues relating to financial markets. Magnus Herweyer provided helpful checking of facts and citations and content feedback. Earlier drafts benefited from the insightful comments of friends, family members, and colleagues, including Tom Adams, Alex Lees, Dave Palmer, Stephen Dobay, Joel Edstrom, and Robert Avanasian. Mary Pons caught numerous errors through her diligent proofreading and editing. Carla King at Author Friendly proved very helpful in bringing the manuscript to completion as a book and bringing the book to market. The entire project benefited from the limitless love, unwavering support, and sharp intellect of my wife, Joanna.

My understanding of Bitcoin and of money in general owes much to great minds who have illuminated these topics with their writing, speech, and actions, including, but not limited to, Andreas Antonopoulos, Nick Szabo, Saifedean Ammous, Wences Casares, John Pfeffer, Pierre Rochard, Michael Goldstein, Jameson Lopp, Andrew Poelstra, Tuur Demeester, Marty Bent, Matt Odell, Stephan Livera, Peter McCormack, Michael Casey, Nic Carter, Ari Paul, Dave Balter, and Pete Mertz.

My understanding also owes much to smart friends who helped me pay attention and get quickly up to speed on Bitcoin, including Alberto Tani and Arun Rao. This manuscript also owes a debt to subject matter experts, including Sam Wald.

Bitcoin itself would not have been possible without the tireless efforts and talents of the Bitcoin software developers, including Satoshi Nakamoto, Hal Finney, and many more too numerous to list.

Undoubtedly this book owes much to people I have neglected to mention. To the accidentally omitted: thank you.

Disclaimers

This book should not be relied on for investment purposes or considered to be investment advice, since every investor's circumstances are different, and Bitcoin and other cryptocurrencies may be inappropriate investments for many people. All readers should do their own analysis or seek appropriate professional advice. This book is not an offer to sell securities of any investment product or any instrument or a solicitation of offers to buy any such securities or instruments. It should not be considered tax advice, since the author is not qualified as a tax advisor. An investment in any strategy, including the discussion of any potential investment strategy described herein, involves a high degree of risk. There is no guarantee that any investments discussed herein will achieve any result. Certain scenarios described herein are for illustrative purposes only. Inclusion of such scenarios is not intended as a recommendation to purchase or sell any investment and performance of these scenarios is not necessarily indicative of what will occur in the market in the future. All investment involves risk, including the loss of principal. Investments in Bitcoin or other cryptocurrencies could result in total loss.

The information in this book is presented for informational purposes only and is believed to be reliable and has been obtained from sources believed to be reliable. However, the author makes no representation as to the accuracy or completeness of such information. Opinions, estimates, and projections in this book constitute the judgment of the author at the time of writing and are subject to change without notice. Any projections, forecasts and estimates contained in this book are necessarily speculative in nature and are based upon certain assumptions. It can be expected that some or all of such assumptions will not materialize or will vary significantly from expectations. Accordingly, any market projections are only estimates, and what happens in the future will differ and may vary substantially from the projections or estimates shown. The author disclaims any obligation to update, modify, or amend this book or to otherwise notify a reader thereof in the event that any matter stated herein, or any opinion, projection, forecast, or estimate set forth herein, changes or subsequently becomes inaccurate.

Certain links, including links to other websites, are provided in this book. These links are provided as a convenience and do not imply the author's sponsorship or approval of any of these websites or their content. The author has no control over or responsibility for other websites that may be accessible from these websites, the contents thereof, their security or privacy policies, or any products/services that may be offered by them. If you access any third-party website through this book you do so at your own risk. Links to or from this book do not constitute an endorsement by the author or the parties or businesses which are so linked, nor do they indicate any affiliation between the author and such parties or businesses. The author owns some well-secured bitcoins as of the writing of this book but makes no representations about such ownership in the future.

Endnotes

[1] *The Economist*, "Mining Digital Gold," 4/13/2013, https://www.economist.com/finance-and-economics/2013/04/13/mining-digital-gold.

[2] *The Wall Street Journal*, "Cryptocurrency Platform Ethereum Gets a Controversial Update," 7/20/2016, Paul Vigna, https://www.wsj.com/articles/cryptocurrency-platform-ethereum-gets-a-controversial-update-1469055722.

[3] *Security Analysis*, Benjamin Graham and David Dodd, 1934.

[4] *Horses in Society: A Story of Animal Breeding and Marketing*, 1800–1920, page 131, Margaret Elsinor Derry, https://books.google.com/books?id=JuJbzVzon44C&pg=PA131&dq=20+million+horses+united+states&hl=en#v=onepage&q=20%20million%20horses%20united%20states&f=false.

[5] *Web Archive*, *"Why most economists' predictions are wrong,"* Paul Krugman, http://web.archive.org/web/19980610100009/www.redherring.com/mag/issue55/economics.html.

[6] *An Inquiry into the Nature and Causes of the Wealth of Nations*, Adam Smith, page 37, https://www.ibiblio.org/ml/libri/s/SmithA_WealthNations_p.pdf.

[7] *Debt: The First 5,000 Years*, David Graeber, pages 21–41.

[8] *International Monetary Fund*, https://www.imf.org/external/pubs/ft/fandd/2007/06/basics.htm.

[9] *Journal of Human Evolution*, Volume 22, Issue 6, June 1992, pages 469–493, Robin Dunbar, https://www.sciencedirect.com/science/article/pii/004724849290081J?via%3Dihub.

[10] *Unenumerated, "Money, blockchains, and social scalability,"* Nick Szabo, http://unenumerated.blogspot.com/2017/02/money-blockchains-and-social-scalability.html.

[11] *Human Action*, Ludwig von Mises, 1949, pages 260, 261, 398, https://mises.org/sites/default/files/Human%20Action_3.pdf.

[12] *On the Origins of Money*, Economic Journal, page 15, 1892, Carl Menger, https://mises-media.s3.amazonaws.com/On%20the%20Origins%20of%20Money_5.pdf.

[13] *On the Origins of Money*, Economic Journal, page 20, 1892, Carl Menger, https://mises-media.s3.amazonaws.com/On%20the%20Origins%20of%20Money_5.pdf.

[14] *The Bitcoin Standard*, Saifedean Ammous, page 2.

[15] *Merriam Webster*, https://www.merriam-webster.com/dictionary/fiat.

[16] *What has Government Done to our Money?*, pages 39–45, Murray N. Rothbard, https://mises-me-dia.s3.amazonaws.com/What%20Has%20Government%20Done%20to%20Our%20Money_3.pdf.

[17] *The New York Times*, "America's Hidden Credit Card Bill," 7/31/2014, Laurence J. Ko-tlikoff, https://www.nytimes.com/2014/08/01/opinion/laurence-kotlikoff-on-fiscal-gap-accounting.html?hp=&action=click&pgtype=Homepage&module=c-column-top-

span-region&region=c-column-top-span-region&WT.nav=c-column-top-span-region%20&_r=0.

[18] *Congressional Budget Office*, "The Budget and Economic Outlook: 2019 to 2029," 1/28/2019, CBO, https://www.cbo.gov/publication/54918.

[19] *The Washington Post*, "U.S. student loan debt reaches a staggering $1.53 trillion," 10/3/2018, Michelle Singletary, https://www.washingtonpost.com/business/2018/10/04/us-student-loan-debt-reaches-staggering-trillion/?utm_term=.1dbf2257d09a.

[20] *Jerome Levy Economics Institute of Bard College*, "The Financial Instability Hypothesis," May 1992, Hyman Minsky, http://www.levyinstitute.org/pubs/wp74.pdf.

[21] *CFA Institute*, https://www.cfainstitute.org/membership/professional-development/refresher-readings/2019/discounted-dividend-valuation.

[22] *Board of Governors of the Federal Reserve System*, "The Discount Rate," https://www.federalreserve.gov/monetarypolicy/discountrate.htm.

[23] *The Great Crash*, pages 137–139, 1929, John Kenneth Galbraith.

[24] *Financial Times*, October 22, 2003, John Kay.

[25] *Wikipedia*, "Mead Westvaco," https://en.wikipedia.org/wiki/MeadWestvaco.

[26] *The Street*, "Goldman Hits Paydirt With Verso, NewPage Deal," 1/8/2014, Antoine Gara, https://www.thestreet.com/story/12218847/1/goldman-hits-paydirt-with-verso-newpage-deal.html.

[27] *Government Publishing Office, The Financial Crisis Inquiry Report*, page 243, https://www.govinfo.gov/content/pkg/GPO-FCIC/pdf/GPO-FCIC.pdf.

[28] *Securities and Exchange Commission*, "Goldman Sachs to Pay Record $550 Million to Settle SEC Charges Related to Subprime Mortgage CDO," 7/15/2010, SEC, https://www.sec.gov/news/press/2010/2010-123.htm.

[29] *Government Publishing Office, The Financial Crisis Inquiry Report*, Page 65, https://www.govinfo.gov/content/pkg/GPO-FCIC/pdf/GPO-FCIC.pdf.

[30] *The New York Times*, "Foreclosures (2012 Robosigning and Mortgage Servicing Settlement)," https://www.nytimes.com/topic/subject/foreclosures-2012-robosigning-and-mortgage-servicing-settlement.

[31] *The Council on Foreign Relations*, "Understanding the Libor Scandal," 10/12/2016, James McBride, https://www.cfr.org/backgrounder/understanding-libor-scandal.

[32] *USA Today*, "3 banks to pay $46.6M for alleged 'spoofing' trading scam," 1/29/2018, Kevin McCoy, https://www.usatoday.com/story/money/2018/01/29/3-banks-pay-46-6-m-alleged-spoofing-trading-scam/1075960001/.

[33] *CNBC*, "Barclays, Citigroup and JP Morgan among banks fined $1.2 billion for forex rigging," 5/16/2019, Spriha Srivastava, https://www.cnbc.com/2019/05/16/eu-regulators-fine-five-banks-for-forex-rigging.html.

[34] *CNN Business*, "The two-year Wells Fargo horror story just won't end," 9/7/2018, Matt Egan, https://money.cnn.com/2018/09/07/news/companies/wells-fargo-scandal-two-years/index.html.

[35] See further discussion in Chapter 8.

[36] *Reuters*, "Banks paid $321 billion in fines since financial crisis: BCG," 3/2/2017, Vishaka George, https://www.reuters.com/article/us-banks-fines/banks-paid-321-billion-in-fines-since-financial-crisis-bcg-idUSKBN1692Y2.

[37] *Lavin*, "Rolling Stone's Matt Taibbi: Is Wall Street Basically Organized Crime?" 4/19/2012, Griftopia, https://www.thelavinagency.com/news/rolling-stone-s-matt-taibbi-is-wall-street-basically-organized-crime.

[38] *Wikipedia*, https://en.wikipedia.org/wiki/Robert_Rubin.

[39] *The New York Times*, "Rubin Leaving Citigroup; Smith Barney for Sale," 1/9/2009, Eric Dash and Louise Story, https://www.nytimes.com/2009/01/10/business/10rubin.html?_r=1&hp.

[40] *Forbes*, "A Loophole for Poor Mr. Paulson," 6/2/2006, Jessica Holzer, https://www.forbes.com/2006/06/01/paulson-tax-loophole-cx_jh_0602paultax.html#11cc6f1065b8.

[41] *Poor Charlie's Almanack*, "The Wit and Wisdom of Charles T. Munger," Page 57, Peter D. Kaufman.

[42] *Mises Institute*, "Socialism: An Economic and Sociological Analysis," 6/15/1951, Ludwig von Mises, https://mises.org/library/socialism-economic-and-sociological-analysis.

[43] *EconLib*, "The Use of Knowledge in Society," September 1945, Friedrich A. Hayek, https://www.econlib.org/library/Essays/hykKnw.html.

[44] *An Inquiry into the Nature and Causes of the Wealth of Nations*, page 349, Adam Smith, https://www.ibiblio.org/ml/libri/s/SmithA_WealthNations_p.pdf.

[45] *The General Theory of Employment, Interest and Money*, John Maynard Keynes, 1936.

[46] *Federal Reserve Bank of Richmond*, "The Federal Reserve's 'Dual Mandate': The Evolution of an Idea," December 2011, Aaron Steelman, https://www.richmondfed.org/-/media/richmondfedorg/publications/research/economic_brief/2011/pdf/eb_11-12.pdf.

[47] *Federal Reserve Bank of Cleveland*, "PCE and CPI Inflation: What's the Difference?" 4/17/2014, FED, https://www.clevelandfed.org/newsroom-and-events/publications/economic-trends/2014-economic-trends/et-20140417-pce-and-cpi-inflation-whats-the-difference.aspx.

[48] *World Trade Organization*, "China," https://www.wto.org/english/thewto_e/acc_e/a1_chine_e.htm.

[49] *The Economist*, "A Tightening Grip: The Future of Factory Asia," 3/12/15, https://www.economist.com/briefing/2015/03/12/a-tightening-grip.

[50] *Centers for Medicare and Medicaid Services*, "Historical," 12/11/2018, https://www.cms.gov/research-statistics-data-and-systems/statistics-trends-and-reports/nationalhealthexpenddata/nationalhealthaccountshistorical.html.

[51] *The Economist*, "America is a health-care outlier in the developed world," 4/26/2016, https://www.economist.com/special-report/2018/04/26/america-is-a-health-care-outlier-in-the-developed-world.

[52] *The Economist*, "America's big spending on health care doesn't pay off," 11/16/2015, https://www.economist.com/united-states/2015/11/16/americas-big-spending-on-health-care-doesnt-pay-off.

[53] *Federal Reserve Bank of St. Louis*, https://fred.stlouisfed.org/series/RHORUSQ156N.

[54] *United States Census Bureau*, https://factfinder.census.gov/faces/tableservices/jsf/pages/productview.xhtml?pid=ACS_17_SPL_K202508&prodType=table.

[55] *Bureau of Labor Statistics*, https://www.bls.gov/cpi/tables/relative-importance/2018.pdf.

[56] *Federal Reserve Bank of St. Louis*, https://fred.stlouisfed.org/series/SPCS20RSA.

[57] *Federal Reserve Bank of St. Louis*, https://fred.stlouisfed.org/series/CPIHOSNS.

[58] *Federal Reserve Bank of St. Louis*, https://fred.stlouisfed.org/series/CSUSHPINSA

[59] *Bureau of Labor Statistics*, https://www.bls.gov/opub/btn/volume-2/pdf/owners-equivalent-rent-and-the-consumer-price-index-30-years-and-counting.pdf

[60] *Board of Governors of the Federal Reserve System*, "What is inflation and how does the Federal Reserve evaluate changes in the rate of inflation?" 9/9/2016, FED, https://www.federalreserve.gov/faqs/economy_14419.htm

[61] *The Washington Post*, "U.S. student loan debt reaches a staggering $1.53 trillion," 10/3/2018, Michelle Singletary, https://www.washingtonpost.com/business/2018/10/04/us-student-loan-debt-reaches-staggering-trillion/?utm_term=.1dbf2257d09a

[62] *National Center for Educational Statistics*, https://nces.ed.gov/fastfacts/display.asp?id=40

[63] *A Template for Understanding Big Debt Crises* by Ray Dalio, page 31

[64] *DNB Working Paper*, no. 632, , "Monetary policy and the top one percent: Evidence from a century of modern economic history," April 2019, Mehdi El Herradi and Aurélien Leroy, https://www.dnb.nl/en/binaries/Working%20paper%20No.%20632_tcm47-383633.pdf

[65] *The Economist*, "Not keeping up with the Joneses - Rising inequality could explain tepid support for redistribution," 4/4/2019, https://www.economist.com/finance-and-economics/2019/04/04/rising-inequality-could-explain-tepid-support-for-redistribution.

[66] *Barron's*, "Ruchir Sharma on Why You Should Buy Emerging Market Stocks," 4/4/2019, Reshma Kapadia, https://www.barrons.com/articles/ruchir-sharma-on-why-you-should-buy-emerging-market-stocks-51554373800.

[67] *Debt: The First 5,000 Years*, David Graeber, page 82.

[68] *The Washington Post*, "Ocasio-Cortez's 70-percent tax rate: Not so radical?" 1/31/2019, Glenn Kessler, https://www.washingtonpost.com/politics/2019/01/31/ocasio-cortezs-percent-tax-rate-not-so-radical/?noredirect=on&utm_term=.501385439495.

[69] *Financial Deepening in Economic Development*, Edward Shaw, 1973.

[70] *Money and Capital in Economic Development*, Ronald McKinnon, 1973.

[71] *Trading Economics*, https://tradingeconomics.com/china/deposit-interest-rate.

[72] *Board of Governors of the Federal Reserve System*, "Federal Reserve issues FOMC statement," 5/1/2019, FED, https://www.federalreserve.gov/newsevents/pressreleases/monetary20190501a.htm.

[73] *Bloomberg Businessweek*, "Warren Buffett Hates It. AOC Is for It. A Beginner's Guide to Modern Monetary Theory," 3/21/2019, Peter Coy, Katia Dmitrieva, and Matthew Boesler, https://www.bloomberg.com/news/features/2019-03-21/modern-monetary-theory-beginner-s-guide.

[74] *Bullion Vault*, "Aristotle's Good Money," 5/1/2009, John Lee, https://www.bullionvault.com/gold-news/money_aristotle_050120092.

[75] *Business Wire*, "History Shows Price of an Ounce of Gold Equals Price of a Decent Men's Suit, Says Sionna Investment Managers," 8/19/2011, Business Wire, https://www.businesswire.com/news/home/20110819005774/en/History-Shows-Price-Ounce-Gold-Equals-Price.

[76] *Unenumerated*, "Antiques, time, gold, and bit gold," 8/28/2008, Unenumerated blog, https://unenumerated.blogspot.com/2005/10/antiques-time-gold-and-bit-gold.html.

[77] *Whither Gold?*, 10/2/1996, Antal Fekete,
http://professorfekete.com/articles/AEFWhitherGold.pdf.

[78] *The Bitcoin Standard*, Saifedean Ammous, page 24.

[79] *The dollar's international role: An "exorbitant privilege"?* 1/7/2016, Ben Bernanke,
https://www.brookings.edu/blog/ben-bernanke/2016/01/07/the-dollars-international-role-an-exorbitant-privilege-2/.

[80] *The New York Times*, "Elizabeth Warren Wants a Wealth Tax. How Would That Even Work?" 2/18/2019, Neil Irwin,
https://www.nytimes.com/2019/02/18/upshot/warren-wealth-tax.html.

[81] *La Nature du Commerce en General*, Part 2, Chapter 7, https://mises.org/library/essay-economic-theory-2.

[82] *Human Action*, page 552, 1949, Ludwig von Mises,
https://mises.org/sites/default/files/Human%20Action_3.pdf.

[83] *Federal Reserve Bank of St. Louis*, https://fredblog.stlouisfed.org/2018/06/paying-interest-on-excess-reserves/.

[84] *The Wall Street Journal*, "Bank sues New York Fed for lack of account," 9/5/2018, Michael S. Derby, https://www.wsj.com/articles/bank-sues-new-york-fed-over-lack-of-account-1536185523.

[85] *Bloomberg*, "The Fed Versus the Narrow Bank," 3/8/2019, Matt Levine,
https://www.bloomberg.com/opinion/articles/2019-03-08/the-fed-versus-the-narrow-bank.

[86] *The New York Times*, "Why Software is Eating the World," 8/20/2011, Marc Andreessen,
https://www.wsj.com/articles/SB10001424053111903480904576512250915629460.

[87] *The Internet of Money*, Andreas Antonopoulos, 2016.

[88] *The Times of London*, "Bitcoin will become the world's single currency, Twitter chief says," 3/2/2018, Alexandra Frean, https://www.thetimes.co.uk/article/bitcoin-will-become-the-worlds-single-currency-tech-chief-says-66slm0p6b.

[89] For readers interested in a more detailed and technical explanation of Bitcoin, I recommend Pedro Franco's book *Understanding Bitcoin*, Kalle Rosenbaum's *Grokking Bitcoin*, and Andreas Antonopoulos' *Mastering Bitcoin*.

[90] There is currently a proposal to switch from the ECDSA digital signature system to a similar (but in some ways better) system called Schnorr. It seems reasonably likely that Schnorr will be implemented due to some of its superior characteristics, and it appears that the reason Bitcoin's signature system was not originally based on Schnorr is that Schnorr was under patent protection until 2008. Given that Schnorr therefore hadn't been tested nearly as much as ECDSA, it seems that Bitcoin's creator chose the safer option. Discussion of Schnorr and the proposal can be found at the following URLs. https://en.wikipedia.org/wiki/Schnorr_signature ; http://diyhpl.us/wiki/transcripts/sf-bitcoin-meetup/2018-07-09-taproot-schnorr-signatures-and-sighash-noinput-oh-my/.

[91] *Bitcoin: A Peer-to-Peer Electronic Cash System*, Satoshi Nakamoto,
https://bitcoin.org/bitcoin.pdf.

[92] *Where Wizards Stay up Late*, 1996, Katie Hafner and Matthew Lyon.

[93] *Cryptoassets*, page 35, 2017, Chris Burniske & Jack Tatar.

[94] *Andy Kessler*, https://www.andykessler.com/about.html.

95 *The Wall Street Journal*, "The Bitcoin Valuation Bubble," 8/27/2017, Andy Kessler, https://www.wsj.com/articles/the-bitcoin-valuation-bubble-1503868225.

96 *The Wall Street Journal*, "Letters to the Editor, Bitcoin Can Be a Competitive Store of Value," 9/13/2017, https://www.wsj.com/articles/bitcoin-can-be-a-competitive-store-of-value-1505231277.

97 *CreditCards.com*, "Rate survey: Average card APR remains at record high of 17.76 percent," 7/3/2019, Kelly Dilworth, https://www.creditcards.com/credit-card-news/rate-report.php.

98 *Forbes*, "Mastercard, AmEx And Envestnet Profit From $400M Business Of Selling Transaction Data," 7/22/2018, Peter Cohan, https://www.forbes.com/sites/petercohan/2018/07/22/mastercard-amex-and-envestnet-profit-from-400m-business-of-selling-transaction-data/#2d40cf0a7722.

99 *Visa*, "Small Business Retail," https://usa.visa.com/run-your-business/small-business-tools/retail.html.

100 *Visa*, "What you need to know about one of the largest world's payment companies," June 2018, https://usa.visa.com/dam/VCOM/download/corporate/media/visanet-technology/aboutvisafactsheet.pdf.

101 *The Curse of Cash*, Kenneth Rogoff, 2016.

102 *The Case for Electronic Cash*, February 6, 2019, https://coincenter.org/entry/the-case-for-electronic-cash.

103 *The Economist*, "The dire consequences of India's demonetization initiative," 12/3/2016, https://www.economist.com/finance-and-economics/2016/12/03/the-dire-consequences-of-indias-demonetisation-initiative.

104 *The Economist*, "The high economic costs of India's demonetization," 1/7/2017, https://www.economist.com/finance-and-economics/2017/01/07/the-high-economic-costs-of-indias-demonetisation.

105 *Pew Research Center*, "Public Trust in Government: 1958-2019," 3/11/2019, https://www.people-press.org/2017/12/14/public-trust-in-government-1958-2017/.

106 *The Washington Post*, "Nine facts about terrorism in the United States since 9/11," 9/11/2013, Brad Plumer, https://www.washingtonpost.com/news/wonk/wp/2013/09/11/nine-facts-about-terrorism-in-the-united-states-since-911/?noredirect=on&utm_term=.34759698a687.

107 *CNN*, "FBI official, dead of 9/11-related cancer, remembered as number of cases grows," 6/18/2018, David Shortell and Nadia Kounang, https://www.cnn.com/2018/06/18/health/9-11-fbi-cancer/index.html.

108 *Watson Institute of International and Public Affairs*, Brown University, "Human Cost of the Post-9/11 Wars: Lethality and the Need for Transparency," November 2018, Neta C. Crawford, https://watson.brown.edu/costsofwar/files/cow/imce/papers/2018/Human%20Costs%2C%20Nov%208%202018%20CoW.pdf.

109 *Watson Institute of International and Public Affairs*, Brown University, "Costs of War," https://watson.brown.edu/costsofwar/.

110 *United States Congress*, "USA Patriot Act of 2001," https://www.congress.gov/bill/107th-congress/house-bill/3162/text/enr.

[111] *United Nations*, "Inclusive Finance," https://www.un.org/esa/ffd/topics/inclusive-local-finance/inclusive-finance.html.

[112] *FDIC*, "FDIC National Survey of Unbanked and Underbanked Households," 10/2018, https://www.fdic.gov/householdsurvey/2017/2017execsumm.pdf.

[113] *Internet World Stats*, https://www.internetworldstats.com/emarketing.htm.

[114] *World Bank*, https://data.worldbank.org/indicator/it.net.user.zs.

[115] *The Economist*, "The past decade has brought a compliance boom in banking," 5/2/2019, https://www.economist.com/finance-and-economics/2019/05/02/the-past-decade-has-brought-a-compliance-boom-in-banking.

[116] *Statista*, "Leading banks in the United States as of December 31, 2018, by number of employees," 5/6/2019, M. Szmigiera, https://www.statista.com/statistics/250220/ranking-of-united-states-banks-by-number-of-employees-in-2018.

[117] *Statista*, "Leading banks in Europe 2018, by total assets (in billion euros)," 6/27/2019, James Cherowbrier, https://www.statista.com/statistics/383406/leading-europe-banks-by-total-assets/.

[118] *The New York Times*, "HSBC to Pay Record Fine to Settle Money-Laundering Charges," 12/11/2012, Jessica Silver-Greenberg, https://dealbook.nytimes.com/2012/12/11/hsbc-to-pay-record-fine-to-settle-money-laundering-charges/.

[119] *Statement of Facts*, Page 17, https://www.justice.gov/sites/default/files/opa/legacy/2012/12/11/dpa-attachment-a.pdf.

[120] *United States Department of Justice*, "BNP Paribas Agrees to Plead Guilty and to Pay $8.9 Billion for Illegally Processing Financial Transactions for Countries Subject to U.S. Economic Sanctions," 6/30/2014, Department of Justice, https://www.justice.gov/opa/pr/bnp-paribas-agrees-plead-guilty-and-pay-89-billion-illegally-processing-financial.

[121] *CNN Money*, "European bank caught laundering Mexican drug money," 2/8/2012, Ivana Kottasova, https://money.cnn.com/2018/02/08/news/rabobank-mexico-drug-money-laundering/index.html.

[122] *The Guardian*, "Standard Chartered fined $1.1bn for money-laundering and sanctions breaches," 4/9/2019, Kalyeena Makortoff, https://www.theguardian.com/business/2019/apr/09/standard-chartered-fined-money-laundering-sanctions-breaches.

[123] *Financial Times*, "Danske: Anatomy of a Money Laundering Scandal," 12/19/2018, https://www.ft.com/content/519ad6ae-bcd8-11e8-94b2-17176fbf93f5.

[124] *The Wall Street Journal*, "Swedbank Ousts CEO Amid Money-Laundering Scandal," 3/28/2019, Patricia Kowsmann and Drew Hinshaw, https://www.wsj.com/articles/swedbank-ousts-ceo-amid-money-laundering-scandal-11553766214.

[125] *United Nations Office on Drugs and Crime (UNODC) website*, https://www.unodc.org/unodc/en/money-laundering/globalization.html.

[126] *The New York Times*, "Bitcoin has Saved My Family," 2/23/2019, Carlos Hernández, https://www.nytimes.com/2019/02/23/opinion/sunday/venezuela-bitcoin-inflation-cryptocurrencies.html.

[127] *Blockchain Revolution*, pages 20 and 183, 2016, Don Tapscott and Alex Tapscott

[128] *The Economist*, "Making remittances cheaper - The cost of cross-border payments needs to drop," 4/11/2019, https://www.economist.com/leaders/2019/04/13/the-cost-of-cross-border-payments-needs-to-drop.

[129] *Bill Barhydt*, https://www.linkedin.com/in/billbar.

[130] *ABRA*, "How Abra works tech talk at 2019 MIT Bitcoin Expo," 4/1/2019, Daniel McGlynn, https://www.abra.com/blog/2019-mit-bitcoin-expo/.

[131] *Target Corporate Website*, "Target Provides Update on Data Breach and Financial Performance," 1/10/2014, Target, https://corporate.target.com/press/releases/2014/01/target-provides-update-on-data-breach-and-financia.

[132] *The Washington Post*, "Hacks of OPM databases compromised 22.1 million people, federal authorities say," 7/9/2015, Ellen Nakashima, https://www.washingtonpost.com/news/federal-eye/wp/2015/07/09/hack-of-security-clearance-system-affected-21-5-million-people-federal-authorities-say/?noredirect=on&utm_term=.6898fa66243a.

[133] *CNN Business*, "Every single Yahoo account was hacked - 3 billion in all," 10/4/2017, Selena Larson, https://money.cnn.com/2017/10/03/technology/business/yahoo-breach-3-billion-accounts/index.html.

[134] *The New York Times*, "Marriott Hacking Exposes Data of Up to 500 Million Guests," 11/30/2018, Nicole Perlroth, Amie Tsang and Adam Satariano, https://www.nytimes.com/2018/11/30/business/marriott-data-breach.html.

[135] *The New York Times*, "Equifax Says Cyberattack May Have Affected 143 Million in the U.S.," 10/7/2017, Tara Siegel Bernard, Tiffany Hsu, Nicole Perlroth and Ron Lieber, https://www.nytimes.com/2017/09/07/business/equifax-cyberattack.html.

[136] *Tech Community Microsoft*, "Toward scalable decentralized identifier systems," 5/13/2019, Alex Simmons, https://techcommunity.microsoft.com/t5/Azure-Active-Directory-Identity/Toward-scalable-decentralized-identifier-systems/ba-p/560168.

[137] *Planetary Resources*, https://www.planetaryresources.com/.

[138] *Medium,* "Planting Bitcoin," 10/31/2018, Dan Held, https://medium.com/@danhedl/planting-bitcoin-sound-money-72e80e40ff62.

[139] *Capitalism, Socialism and Democracy*, 1942, Joseph Schumpeter.

[140] *On the Origin of Species*, 1859, Charles Darwin.

[141] *The Journal of Finance*, "Portfolio Selection," March 1952, Harry Markowitz, https://onlinelibrary.wiley.com/doi/full/10.1111/j.1540-6261.1952.tb01525.x.

[142] *Multicoin Capital*, "$100 Trillion," 10/9/2018, Kyle Samani, https://multicoin.capital/2018/10/09/100-trillion/.

[143] *The Money Project*, "All of the World's Money and Markets in One Visualization," 10/26/17, Jeff Desjardins, http://money.visualcapitalist.com/worlds-money-markets-one-visualization-2017/.

[144] *National Bureau of Economic Research*, "Who Owns the Wealth in Tax Havens? Macro Evidence and Implications for Global Inequality," 12/27/2017, Alstadsaeter, Johannesen, Zucman, https://www.nber.org/papers/w23805.pdf.

[145] The Guardian, "Number of empty homes in England rises to more than 216,000," 3/19/2019, Julia Kollewe, https://www.theguardian.com/society/2019/mar/11/empty-homes-england-rises-property.

[146] *Savills.co.uk*, "How much is the world worth?," 4/10/2017, The Savills Blog, https://www.savills.co.uk/blog/article/216300/residential-property/how-much-is-the-world-worth.aspx.

[147] *How Money Got Free*, pages 22–32, 2017, Brian Patrick Eha.

[148] *The Age of Cryptocurrency*, pages 53–57, Paul Vigna and Michael J. Casey.

[149] *The Telegraph*, "Google's ex-CEO predicts that China will cause the internet to 'split in two' by 2028," 9/21/2018, Joseph Archer, https://www.telegraph.co.uk/technology/2018/09/21/googles-ex-ceo-predicts-china-will-cause-internet-split-two/.

[150] *Github*, "Bitcoin Repository," https://github.com/bitcoin/bitcoin.

[151] *Facebook*, "Thanks to everyone who participated in today's round of trivia. Windows XP was compiled of 45 million lines of code. Whoa! What are your favorite memories of Windows XP?," 1/11/2011, Windows Facebook page, https://www.facebook.com/windows/posts/155741344475532.

[152] *Coindesk*, "Bitmain Announces New, More Efficient 7nm Bitcoin Mining Chip," 2/18/2019, Daniel Palmer, https://www.coindesk.com/bitmain-announces-new-more-efficient-7nm-bitcoin-mining-chip.

[153] *Blockchain.info*, "Hashrate Distribution", https://www.blockchain.com/pools

[154] *Betterhash.net*, https://www.betterhash.net/

[155] *Bitnodes*, "Bitnodes home page," https://bitnodes.earn.com/.

[156] *Coindesk*, "Ethereum Classic's Price Stumbles Amid Suspected 51% Attack," 1/7/2019, Sam Ouimet, https://www.coindesk.com/ethereum-classic-price-stumbles-amid-suspected-51-attack.

[157] *Coindesk*, "Verge's Blockchain Attacks Are Worth a Sober Second Look," 6/5/2018, Alyssa Hertig, https://www.coindesk.com/verges-blockchain-attacks-are-worth-a-sober-second-look.

[158] *Federal Reserve*, "Crisis and Calm: Demand for U.S. Currency at Home and Abroad from the Fall of the Berlin Wall to 2011,"November 2012, Ruth Judson, https://www.federalreserve.gov/pubs/ifdp/2012/1058/ifdp1058.pdf.

[159] *Federal Reserve*, "Currency in Circulation: Value," 4/2/2019, FED, https://www.federalreserve.gov/paymentsystems/coin_currcircvalue.htm.

[160] *Federal Reserve*, "How much U.S. currency is in circulation?," 4/2/2019, FED, https://www.federalreserve.gov/faqs/currency_12773.htm.

[161] *The Curse of Cash*, 2016, Kenneth Rogoff.

[162] *Reuters*, "China wants to ban bitcoin mining," 4/8/2019, Brenda Goh, Alun John, https://www.reuters.com/article/us-china-cryptocurrency/china-wants-to-ban-bitcoin-mining-traders-say-move-not-a-surprise-idUSKCN1RL0C4?mod=article_inline.

[163] *Wikipedia*, "Executive Order 6102," https://en.wikipedia.org/wiki/Executive_Order_6102.

[164] *TorrentFreak*, "Netflix Dominates Internet Traffic Worldwide, BitTorrent Ranks Fifth," 11/17/2018, Ernesto, https://torrentfreak.com/netflix-dominates-internet-traffic-worldwide-bittorrent-ranks-.fifth-181116.

165 *Facebook.com*, "A Privacy-Focused Vision for Social Networking," 3/6/2019, Mark Zuckerberg, https://www.facebook.com/notes/mark-zuckerberg/a-privacy-focused-vision-for-social-networking/10156700570096634/.

166 *The Age of Surveillance Capitalism*, 2019, Shoshana Zuboff.

167 *The Age of Surveillance Capitalism*, 2019, Shoshana Zuboff.

168 *Sagepub*, "Increases in Depressive Symptoms, Suicide-Related Outcomes, and Suicide Rates Among U.S. Adolescents After 2010 and Links to Increased New Media Screen Time," 11/14/2017, Jean M. Twenge, Thomas E. Joiner, Megan L. Rogers, Gabrielle N. Martin, https://journals.sagepub.com/doi/abs/10.1177/2167702617723376?journalCode=cpxa.

169 *The Shallows: What the Internet Is Doing to Our Brains*, Nicholas Carr.

170 *The Conversation*, "How Facebook has become the world's largest echo chamber," 2/5/2018, Megan Knight, http://theconversation.com/explainer-how-facebook-has-become-the-worlds-largest-echo-chamber-91024.

171 *The New York Times*, "Russian Influence Reached 126 Million Through Facebook Alone," 10/30/2017, Mike Isaac and Daisuke Wakabayashi, https://www.nytimes.com/2017/10/30/technology/facebook-google-russia.html.

172 *Esquire*, "Silicon Valley's Tax-Avoiding, Job-Killing, Soul-Sucking Machine," 2/8/2018, Scott Galloway, https://www.esquire.com/news-politics/a15895746/bust-big-tech-silicon-valley/.

173 *CNBC*, "More than 200,000 sign petition in South Korea to stop government's crackdown on bitcoin 'happy dream'," 1/16/2018, Evelyn Cheng, https://www.cnbc.com/2018/01/16/over-200000-sign-petition-in-south-korea-to-stop-bitcoin-regulation.html.

174 *Bloomberg*, "Bitcoin Speculators, Not Drug Dealers, Dominate Crypto Use Now," 9/7/2018, Camila Russo, https://www.bloomberg.com/news/articles/2018-08-07/bitcoin-speculators-not-drug-dealers-dominate-crypto-use-now.

175 *Off the Chain Podcast with Anthony Pompliano*, Patrick O'Kain, "Special Agent for the DEA: How Criminals are Using Cryptocurrency," 5/8/2019, https://podcasts.apple.com/us/podcast/patrick-okain-special-agent-for-dea-how-criminals-are/id1434060078?i=1000437505160.

176 https://www.irs.gov/businesses/small-businesses-self-employed/virtual-currencies.

177 https://www.cftc.gov/Bitcoin/index.htm.

178 *Fortune*, "The Feds Just Collected $48 Million from Seized Bitcoins," 10/2/2017, Jeff John Roberts, http://fortune.com/2017/10/02/bitcoin-sale-silk-road/.

179 *United States Treasury Press Releases*, "Treasury Designates Iran-Based Financial Facilitators of Malicious Cyber Activity and for the First Time Identifies Associated Digital Currency Addresses," 11/28/2018, US Treasury, https://home.treasury.gov/news/press-releases/sm556.

180 *CNN*, "90 percent of U.S. bills carry traces of cocaine," 8/17/2009, Madison Park, http://www.cnn.com/2009/HEALTH/08/14/cocaine.traces.money/.

181 *IRS website*, https://www.irs.gov/pub/irs-drop/n-14-21.pdf.

182 *Forbes*, "Bitcoin Virtual Currency Deals Under $600 Could Become Tax Exempt," 9/8/2017, Robert W. Wood,

https://www.forbes.com/sites/robertwood/2017/09/08/bitcoin-virtual-currency-deals-under-600-could-become-tax-exempt/#19401a163bc6.

183 *Union Square Ventures,* "Fat Protocols," 8/8/2016, Joel Monegro, https://www.usv.com/blog/fat-protocols.

184 *Securities and Exchange Commission,* "Staff Letter: Engaging on Fund Innovation and Cryptocurrency-related Holdings," 1/18/2018, Dalia Blass, https://www.sec.gov/divisions/investment/noaction/2018/cryptocurrency-011818.htm.

185 *Securities and Exchange Commission,* "Bitcoin ETF Memorandum," 3/20/2019, SEC, https://www.sec.gov/comments/sr-nysearca-2019-01/srnysearca201901-5164833-183434.pdf.

186 *Coindiligent,* "Satoshi Nakamota's net wealth," 6/19/2019, Nick Dominguez, https://coindiligent.com/satoshi-net-worth.

187 *How Money Got Free,* pages 22–24, 2017, Brian Patrick Eha.

188 *YouTube,* "F.A. Hayek on Monetary Policy, the Gold Standard, Deficits, Inflation, and John Maynard Keynes," 1984, Libertarianism.org, https://www.youtube.com/watch?v=EYhEDxFwFRU#t=19m23s.

189 *Business Insider,* "Amazon Web Services is bigger than its next 4 competitors combined as cloud became a $70 billion market last year," 2/6/2019, Julie Bort, https://www.businessinsider.com/aws-market-share-dominates-70-billion-cloud-market-2019-2.

190 *Time,* "Amazon Has More Than 100 Million Prime Subscribers, Reveals Jeff Bezos," April 19, 2018, Katie Reilly, http://time.com/5245969/amazon-prime-100-million-subscribers-jeff-bezos/.

191 *Facebook Investor Relations, Q1 2019 Earnings,* Slides, page 3, Monthly Active Users, https://s21.q4cdn.com/399680738/files/doc_financials/2019/Q1/Q1-2019-Earnings-Presentation.pdf.

192 *Libra,* https://libra.org/en-US/white-paper/#introducing-libra.

193 *The Economist,* "Young people and their phones are shaking up banking," 5/2/2019, https://www.economist.com/special-report/2019/05/02/young-people-and-their-phones-are-shaking-up-banking.

194 *Libra,* https://libra.org/en-US/white-paper/#introducing-libra.

195 *U.S. House Committee on Financial Services,* 6/18/2018, https://financialservices.house.gov/news/documentsingle.aspx?DocumentID=403943.

196 *ABC News,* "Elizabeth Warren calls to break up Facebook, Google and Amazon", 3/8/2019, Jason Abbruzzese, https://www.nbcnews.com/tech/tech-news/elizabeth-warren-calls-break-facebook-google-amazon-n980911.

197 *The Economist,* 8/15/2018, Across the West powerful firms are becoming even more powerful.

198 *The New York Times,* "Google Fined $1.7 Billion by E.U. for Unfair Advertising Rules," 3/20/2019, Adam Satariano, https://www.nytimes.com/2019/03/20/business/google-fine-advertising.html.

199 *The New York Times,* "Google Fined $1.7 Billion by E.U. for Unfair Advertising Rules," 3/20/2019, Adam Satariano, https://www.nytimes.com/2019/03/20/business/google-fine-advertising.html.

200 *Berkshire Hathaway*, "Berkshire Hathaway 2018 10-K,"
http://www.berkshirehathaway.com/2018ar/201810-k.pdf.

201 *The Guardian*, "Barclays to sell customer data, Bank tells 13 million customers it is to start selling information on their spending habits to other companies," 6/24/2013, Rupert Jones, https://www.theguardian.com/business/2013/jun/24/barclays-bank-sell-customer-data.

202 *Oaktree Capital*, "There They Go Again . . . Again," 9/7/2017, Howard Marks, https://www.oaktreecapital.com/docs/default-source/memos/there-they-go-again-again.pdf?sfvrsn=6.

203 *Oaktree Capital*, "Yet Again?," 9/7/2017, Howard Marks, https://www.oaktreecapital.com/docs/default-source/memos/yet-again.pdf?sfvrsn=6.

204 *The New Republic*, Albert Goldman, Lindy's Law, 6/13/1964, https://www.dropbox.com/s/qripnmgbnvtyx16/1964-goldman.pdf.

205 *The Fractal Geometry of Nature*, 1983, Benoit Mandelbrot, https://books.google.com/books?id=0R2LkE3N7-oC&pg=PA342&lpg=PA342&dq=%22The+fractal+geometry+of+Nature%22+lindy#v=onepage&q=%22The%20fractal%20geometry%20of%20Nature%22%20lindy&f=false.

206 *Antifragile: Things that Gain from Disorder*, Page 318, 2012, Nassim Taleb, https://books.google.com/books?id=5fqbz_qGi0AC&pg=PA318&lpg=PA318&dq=%22If+a+book+has+been+in+print+for+forty+years,+I+can+expect+it+to+be+in+print+for+another+forty+years%22#v=onepage&q=%22another%20forty%20years%22&f=false.

207 *CNBC*, "Like flu season, the 'infectious' spread of bitcoin could be over, Barclays says," 4/10/2018, Kate Rooney, https://www.cnbc.com/2018/04/10/like-flu-season-the-infectious-spread-of-bitcoin-could-be-over-barclays-says.html.

208 *Visual Capitalist*, "The Rising Speed of Technological Adoption," 2/14/2018, Jeff Desjardins, https://www.visualcapitalist.com/rising-speed-technological-adoption/.

209 *Medium*, "Bitcoin is a Demographic Mega-Trend: Data Analysis," 4/30/2019, Spencer Bogart, https://medium.com/blockchain-capital-blog/bitcoin-is-a-demographic-mega-trend-data-analysis-160d2f7731e5.

210 *Wikiquote*, "Max Planck," 4/25/19, https://en.wikiquote.org/wiki/Max_Planck.

211 *United States Department of Defense (DoD)*, "Defense Budget Overview," 2/2/2018, DoD, https://comptroller.defense.gov/Portals/45/Documents/defbudget/fy2019/FY2019_Budget_Request_Overview_Book.pdf.

212 *Life After Google*, George Gilder, 2018.

213 *Coinshares*, "The Bitcoin Mining Network - Trends, Marginal Creation Cost, Electricity Consumption & Sources," 11/26/2018, https://coinshares.co.uk/bitcoin-mining-cost/.

214 *The Wall Street Journal*, "In America's Hottest Drilling Spot, Gas Is Going Up in Smoke," 8/29/2018, Rebecca Elliott, https://www.wsj.com/articles/in-americas-hottest-drilling-spot-vast-volumes-of-gas-go-up-in-smoke-1535535001?mod=article_inline.

215 *The New York Times*, "The Natural Gas Industry Has a Leak Problem," 6/21/2018, John Schwartz and Brad Plumer, https://www.nytimes.com/2018/06/21/climate/methane-leaks.html.

[216] *Nature*, "Methane fluxes show consistent temperature dependence across microbial to ecosystem scales," 3/19/2018, Gabriel Yvon-Durocher, Andrew P. Allen, David Bastviken, Ralf Conrad, Cristian Gudasz, Annick St-Pierre, Nguyen Thanh-Duc & Paul A. del Giorgio, https://www.nature.com/articles/nature13164

[217] *Upstream Data*, https://upstreamdata.ca/home.

[218] *Medium*, "Introducing Bakkt," 8/3/19, Kelly Loeffler, https://medium.com/bakkt-blog/introducing-bakkt-e1794dd3a45d.

[219] *Fortune*, "The NYSE's Owner Wants to Bring Bitcoin to Your 401(k). Are Crypto Credit Cards Next?," 8/3/19, Shawn Tully, http://fortune.com/longform/nyse-owner-bitcoin-exchange-startup/.

[220] *Medium*, "Custody in the Age of Digital Assets," 10/15/19, Fidelity Digital Assets, https://medium.com/@FidelityDigitalAssets/custody-in-the-age-of-digital-assets-95799f347016.

[221] *Fidelity*, "Fidelity by the Numbers: Corporate Statistics," 3/21/19, Fidelity, https://www.fidelity.com/about-fidelity/fidelity-by-numbers/corporate-statistics.

[222] *Fidelity*, "Institutional Investors See a Place for Digital Assets in Investment Portfolios," 5/2/19, Fidelity Digital Assets, https://www.fidelity.com/bin-public/060_www_fidelity_com/documents/press-release/institutional-investments-in-digital-assets-050219.pdf.

[223] *Medium*, "New Research: Institutional Investments Likely to Increase over Next 5 Years," 5/2/19, Fidelity Digital Assets, https://medium.com/@FidelityDigitalAssets/new-research-institutional-investments-likely-to-increase-over-next-5-years-729fb1ca3c52.

Index

Get More On Bitcoin and the Author Here

More Bitcoin and Investing Information

Find insights, news, and answers to your questions about Bitcoin and investing on my website. You can also find where to connect with me on social media and elsewhere. Just visit:

www.andyedstrom.com

Review Why Buy Bitcoin

Was this book helpful? Did you love it? I'd love it if you'd provide a quick review. Here's the link to review the book online. Thank you!

www.andyedstrom.com/books

View the Figures

Here's the link to view the figures on the web in full size.

www.andyedstrom.com/wbb-figures

Made in the USA
Las Vegas, NV
27 February 2021